THE
Kaleidoscope
BOOK

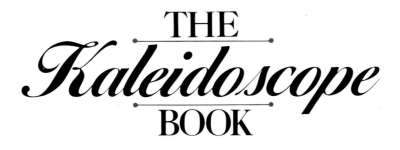

"Jay-Leido," kaleidoscopic drawing by Betty Tribe

THE
Kaleidoscope
BOOK

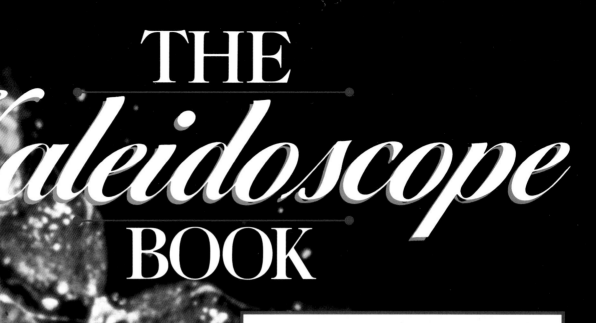

A Spectrum of Spectacular Scopes to Make

Edited by
Thom Boswell

Sterling Publishing Co., Inc.   New York
A STERLING/LARK BOOK

Editing: Thom Boswell
Design: Thom Boswell and Sandra Montgomery
Production: Sandra Montgomery, Elaine Thompson,
   Wendy Wells
Photography: Evan Bracken
Drawings: Sandra Montgomery

ISBN 0-8069-8370-1

Library of Congress Cataloging-in-Publication Data

The kaleidoscope book : a spectrum of spectacular scopes to
make / edited by Thom Boswell.
      p.   cm.
   "A Sterling/Lark book."
   Includes bibliographical references (p.   ) and index.
   ISBN 0-8069-8370-1
   1. Kaleidoscope.   1. Boswell, Thom.
QC373.K3K35   1992
688.7'2--dc20   91-38786
                                                 CIP

10   9   8   7   6   5   4   3

A Sterling/Lark Book

First paperback edition published in 1995 by
   Sterling Publishing Company, Inc.
   387 Park Avenue South, New York, N.Y. 10016

Produced by Altamont Press, Inc.
   50 College Street, Asheville, NC 28801

© 1992 by Altamont Press

Distributed in Canada by Sterling Publishing
   ℅ Canadian Manda Group, One Atlantic Avenue, Suite 105
   Toronto, Ontario, Canada M6K 3E7
Distributed in Great Britain and Europe by Cassell PLC
   Wellington House, 125 Strand, London WC2R 0BB, England
Distributed in Australia by Capricorn Link (Australia) Pty Ltd.
   P.O. Box 6651, Baulkham Hills, Business Centre, NSW 2153, Australia

Every effort has been made to ensure that all the information in
this book is accurate. However, due to differing conditions,
tools, and individual skills, the publisher cannot be responsible for any injuries, losses, and other damages which may
result from the use of the information in this book.

Printed and bound in Hong Kong

Sterling ISBN 0-8069-8370-1 Trade
                0-8069-8371-X Paper

Table of Contents

INTRODUCTION

by Ledell Murphy

Perhaps the magic comes from the perfect blending of art and science in the kaleidoscope, which means an instrument for "viewing beautiful forms." Or perhaps the magic is within each beholder, as we seek beautiful views of the world.

It is exciting for me, as a collector of kaleidoscopes, to share my passion for this magic with you, a potential crafter! My ulterior motive is that, after mastering the basics of kaleidoscope design, you will bring your own talents and imagination to this art form and create new and wonderful scopes for me to add to my collection.

While the primary purpose of this book is to inform you about constructing the physical body of a kaleidoscope, it seems important to balance that information with thoughts about the spirit of the kaleidoscope. After all, kaleidoscopes have to do with symmetry and harmony. So, first we'll take a brief look at the beginnings of the kaleidoscope, as well as the contemporary craze. Then we'll get familiar with the components of a kaleidoscope in a non-technical way, for the purpose of general understanding and vocabulary. We'll also look at some of the ways people view scopes and use them.

Antique reproduction parlor scope by David and Marty Roenigk (opposite).

Stained glass interpretation of a kaleidoscopic image, by Charles Karadimos (right).

HISTORY & CURRENT RENAISSANCE

Sir David Brewster, a Scotsman, first invented the kaleidoscope in 1813, and filed the first patent in 1816. The more I learn about Sir David, the more fitting it seems that he should have developed this wondrous blend of art and science. Sir David was fascinated with science from early childhood, especially with the study of light. His formal education, however, prepared him for the ministry. He was never ordained, but his philosophical beliefs were strongly developed. He was a leading member of the "natural" scientists of the early nineteenth century. One of his tenets was that there need be no conflict between science and religion, and he worked to minimize any such dispute.

Although you may never have heard Sir David's name until now, you are probably familiar with the color wheel. It is Sir David who is credited with identifying red, blue and yellow as the "primary" colors from which all other colors are derived. It was during his experiments with polarized light that he determined this, as well as developed the kaleidoscope.

Sir David earned his living by writing, and by serving as editor of several publications. Although his papers and books, as well as the publications with which he was associated, were scholarly, they were also regarded in a popular vein.

Sir David was not a theorist, but an experimenter. He observed, and tried, and recorded. So as you master the basics of crafting the components of your kaleidoscope, and continue to experiment with variations of the components and with new and different combinations, you can be assured that you are following the approach of the kaleidoscope creator himself.

Technical illustration from Sir David Brewster's 1816 patent on the kaleidoscope.

Kaleidoscopes were instantly successful. Thousands were sold in London and Paris within months, although they were not Sir David's creations. It was called "the great philosophical toy." It seems that from the beginning, people recognized that kaleidoscopes were more than something pretty to look at.

The best known early kaleidoscope maker in America was Charles Green Bush. Prussian by birth, he immigrated to Boston in 1847. His 1873 parlor scope design has been commemorated with reproductions by two contemporary companies. These scopes were often seen in Victorian salons. Bush is best remembered in the kaleidoscope world for "liquid filled ampules." These hand blown tubes were used by Bush as object chamber items, and they created special interest in the images. Only a few contemporary artists have been able to duplicate the process.

More detailed historical information about early kaleidoscope designers, techniques, patents, and uses is available, but is limited. Antique kaleidoscopes, both European and American, are scarce and highly priced.

We all owe a debt of gratitude to the American toy makers, who are principally responsible for keeping kaleidoscopes alive from the early 1900s until the early 1980s. "I haven't seen one of these since I was a kid," is probably the most frequently heard phrase at a showing of contemporary scopes. Many of us recall those childhood memories of kaleidoscopes. And we somehow recapture that childlike sense of wonder and awe once we have occasion to view contemporary kaleidoscopes.

Although there were several kaleidoscope artists on the scene as early as the 1960s and '70s, if there is one person to be credited with

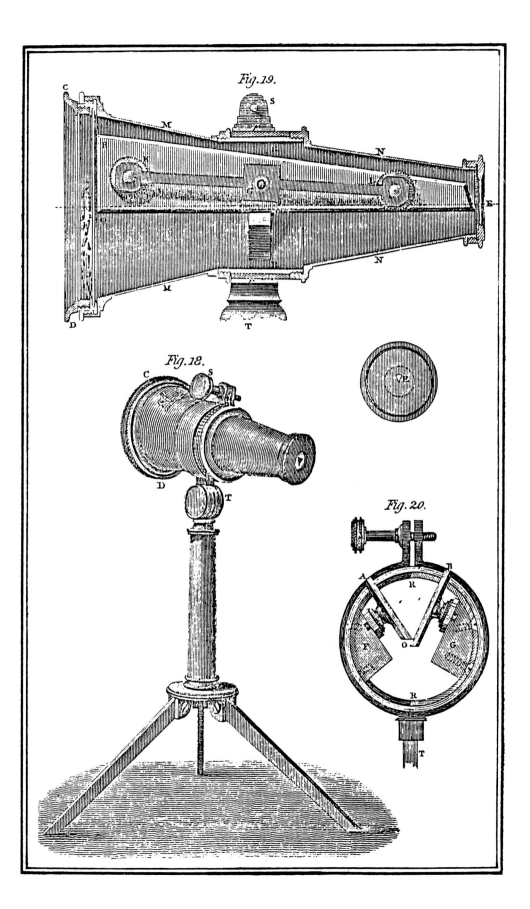

Fig.19.

Fig.18.

Fig.20.

Antique scopes (opposite top), old toy scopes (right) and contemporary scopes (opposite bottom), all from the vast collection of Cozy Baker at Strathmore Hall.

One section of scopes from the collection of Tess & Marty Scherer, the Scherer Gallery (below).

the re-emergence of the kaleidoscope as an important art form, it is Cozy Baker. This warm, energetic, lively, and multi-faceted woman has shared her love for kaleidoscopes with the world. In her 1985 book, *Through the Kaleidoscope*, Cozy introduced us to more than 40 artists then actively making and marketing kaleidoscopes. She also curated the first exhibition of kaleidoscopes in America at Strathmore Hall in suburban Washington, D.C. In 1986, Cozy formed the Brewster Society, gathering together the "designers, collectors, and lovers of kaleidoscopes." The Kaleidoscope Renaissance was underway. The following year, so much had happened in the kaleido-world that Cozy updated her book, issuing it as *Through the Kaleidoscope... And Beyond.* Nearly 100 artists were featured. In 1990, Cozy gave us *KALEIDORAMA*, a fun and fanciful book. There has been a calendar, many articles in periodicals, national news features, philanthropic donations of scopes, gallery shows, museum exhibits, national conventions, and regional gatherings—all because this woman took her talents and know-how, combined them with her passion for kaleidoscopes, brought together kindred spirits, and shared these wonderful "philosophical toys" as they re-emerged in the art world. The kaleido-community that Cozy has fostered has a synergy as wonderful as kaleidoscopes themselves. By encouraging new artists and promoting the highest quality scopes with collectors and galleries, the art form has blossomed and grown. And the spirits of many participants have been individually nurtured while melding into a living kaleidoscope.

One factor that new kaleidoscope makers should be aware of is the high ethical standards that knit the kaleido-community together. Most of the kaleidoscopes you see in books, articles, galleries and shows are copyrighted or patent-ed. There is important legal and moral respect for the "ownership" of the concepts that have been developed. This ethical concern is shared by collectors and gallery owners as well.

The number of artists, and collectors, continuously increases, and the variety of wonderful scopes now available is astonishing. But at any gathering of kaleido-crazies, ideas are generated for more scopes than anyone has yet had time to produce. There is a place for you.

COMPONENTS

Sir David wrote that not one in a thousand makers, nor one in ten thousand viewers, of kaleidoscopes would know or understand the optical principles on which they are based. He seemed to want us to enjoy them anyway, so this non-technical description of the components may be enough for most of you. However, more technical information appears later in the book, and those of you who want to learn the physics may be even more creative in the designs of your own scopes.

Although there are generally four basic components of a kaleidoscope (eye piece, external presentation, mirror system, and object chamber), there are many variations of each of these components—and new variations waiting to be implemented by you. The variations of these individual components, along with a few other design considerations (such as objects in the chamber and light source), can be combined in limitless ways to create new and wonderful scopes.

The Kaleidoscopic Image

It's often difficult to know where to begin, but in this case it seems obvious to begin at the end. It is impossible to discuss the various components without first discussing the goal.

"Krystoscope," kaleidoscopic art (originally in color)
rendered by **Betty Tribe.**

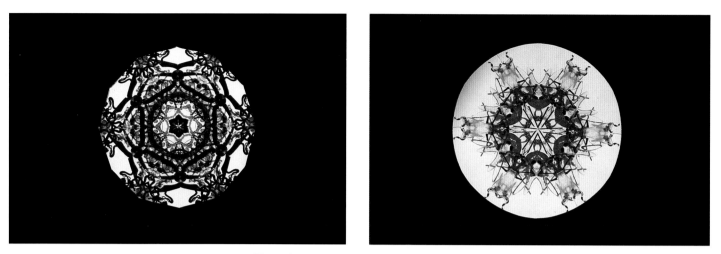

Two-mirror images, by Charles Karadimos

Three-mirror images, by Carolyn Bennett

Computer generated images, by Karl Schilling

"Irribundance 40, " kaleidoscopic drawing by **Betty Tribe,** commissioned by the **Irrigation Association** (courtesy of **Hunter Industries).**

In each decision you make about how you want to vary the mirror system, or object chamber, or objects, or even in how you want to present your scope, the ultimate goal is to produce wondrous images. After all, Brewster chose the name "kaleidoscope" to describe an instrument for viewing beautiful forms. While the presentation may be wondrous to behold, and sculptural art in itself, what makes it a kaleidoscope is its beautiful images.

You have seen examples of kaleidoscope images in some quilt patterns, in snowflakes, in tie-dyeing patterns, and in fireworks displays. There are two common images. (See photos on page 14.) One is a "mandala": a circular, snowflake-like pattern that appears at the end of the barrel. The other type fills your entire field of vision. Both are comprised of three-sided replications of the objects in the object chamber. Both have rhythm and harmony and intricacies. Each has visual integrity and impact.

People often have preferences for one or the other. Many kaleidoscope artists make scopes that produce both types of image. There are even artists that combine two different mirror systems in the same kaleidoscope so that you can look at either image type. And there are other mirror designs which produce further variations of image patterns.

There is special magic in a kaleidoscopic image. The colors, shapes, forms, and patterns combine in ever-changing, seldom-repeating relationships. The kaleidoscopic mandala has been called a metaphor for the New Age. The image can be thought of as the world, with diversity in its pieces, but unification when viewed in its totality. The image can be thought of as life, filled with unexpected beauty to be enjoyed. And just as Nature is filled with symmetry and balance, so are the images created by you in your kaleidoscope.

External Presentation

The simplest way to think of the external presentation is how the kaleidoscope might look displayed on a coffee table. Although the other components could conceivably be held together with masking tape, and still have the most beautiful images imaginable, they wouldn't be very attractive from the outside. So a pleasing exterior becomes important.

Your childhood memory of a kaleidoscope may be of a cardboard tube, 6 to 8 inches in length, and 1 to 3 inches in diameter. The tube you remember may have been covered in colorful paper, perhaps with a theme. Toy makers and contemporary scope artists still offer wonderful pieces in cardboard tubes.

But it is in the external presentation that the most obvious variety occurs. In general, scope makers bring their previous artistic talents and skills to the presentation of their scopes. For example, stained glass artists who begin making scopes might offer a stained glass housing, using wonderful colors, patterns and textures of glass to make the piece beautiful to look at from the outside. Woodworkers may offer a lathe-turned barrel, perhaps with inlay. Metalworkers might use hammered brass or silver, decorated with an enameled design. A whimsical sense of humor can also be exercised by creating scopes with presentations that are pure fun.

External presentations can sometimes be of equal importance to the images inside. Some scopes are offered in fantasy settings, complete with flowing water and sparkling external lights. Some are offered in large abstract architectural shapes. One scope maker has joined with a sculptor to incorporate a scope into cast figures of very large scale. Another designer, who raises prize poultry, uses goose eggs for her presentation.

Whatever talents and skills and interests you already have can be used to create your own exterior. I have yet to see stiffened crochet, bread dough sculpture, embroidery, basketry, quilting, scrimshaw, or corn husks used as exteriors. Your own kaleidoscope's design is an opportunity to re-apply your current passions to another art form.

There are a few considerations in the external presentations. Is your scope to be a parlor scope or handheld? A parlor scope usually sits at an angle on an arm attached to a

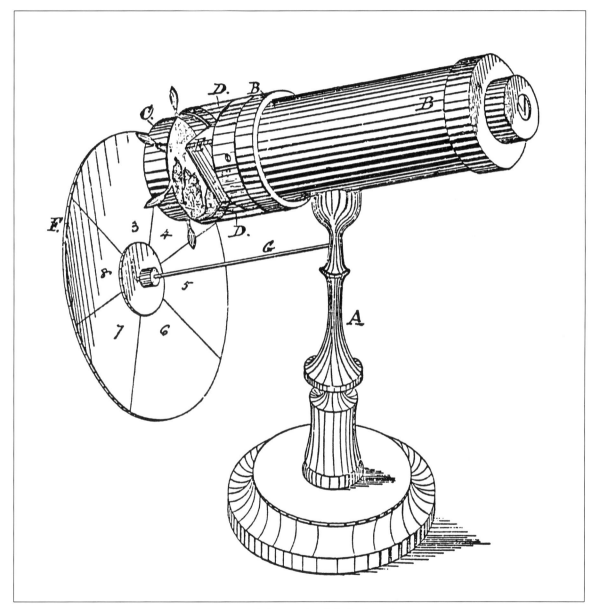

Patent illustration of the popular C.G. Bush parlor scope.

base. It can be viewed without lifting it. This would be important for very heavy or very large scopes. Occasionally the scope itself is detachable for use as a handheld scope. Often a handheld is accompanied by some (usually small) stand to use for displaying it—and to keep it from rolling off the table.

Another consideration is size. Lengths and diameters range from 1-inch miniatures to the world's largest, over 12 feet. You may want your scope to be wearable. Some artists offer scopes as fine pieces of jewelry—pendants for a chain, tie tacks, bracelets, and rings.

Often there is some coordination of the exterior presentation with the images created inside. This coordination may be in the color scheme used, thematic motifs, or in the general "feel" of the scope.

Your chosen mirror system and object chamber may dictate some size and shape parameters for the external presentation. Or you may know how you want the exterior to look, thereby placing some limitations on the other components. It's one of those "which came first, the chicken or the egg," questions. And there is no rule.

As you perfect your kaleidoscope construction skills and critique your own work, or as you look at kaleidoscopes in galleries and shops, you may want to consider evaluating the external presentation in terms of workmanship. In selecting a new scope for my collection, it is important to me that the workmanship be of the highest quality. Attractive and pleasing appearance are matters of personal choice, of course. Another of my considerations is how comfortable the scope is to hold and view for extended periods of time.

Mirror Systems

It is the mirror system of a kaleidoscope that creates the magic. The mirror shape, the number of mirrors used, and the angle(s) at which the mirrors are joined combine to produce the pattern of image you see. The toy scopes we remember were generally made with highly polished metal, not glass mirrors, in a straight shape, two-mirror, 60° angle system. This produces a mandala: a single, symmetrical, circular "snowflake" at the end of the tube. The other most popular system is three straight mirrors in an equilateral triangle. This system produces a faceted pattern that fills the entire field of view.

There are other variations using four or more mirrors, tapering the mirrors, and circular systems using flexible, reflective materials. Some artists are making poly-angular mirror systems. That is, there is a mechanism that allows the two-mirror system's angle to be altered. Other variations include altering the angle(s) at which the mirrors are placed. Narrower angles increase the number of replications, which, in general, add to the complexity of the image. There is opportunity with the mirror system for much experimentation.

When I evaluate a kaleidoscope, I look closely at the mirror system. Dust particles or fingerprints are not acceptable. And I look for a mirror system that is sealed to prevent dust and dirt from entering it. Quality kaleidoscopes are made with first- (or front-) surface mirrors. These have the reflective coating on the top surface of the glass rather than behind the glass, as is the case with most common mirrors. First-surface mirrors give a sharper, truer image. They are also more expensive. An invisible seam where the mirrors join is difficult to accomplish, but is an indication of highest quality workmanship. I also evaluate the mirror system implementation by looking closely at the image. The mirror system should create regularity in the pattern replication. The symmetry should be perfect, or near perfect, with certain angles, and have no distracting diversion along the pattern lines.

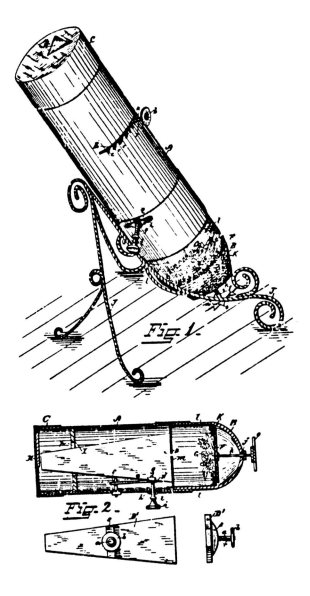

Drawing of kaleidoscope patented by R. Leach, 1885.

Object Chamber

The object chamber is also referred to as the "cell." It is the object chamber that holds the objects you choose to replicate with your mirror system. Some scopes have no object chamber and no objects. These are called teleidoscopes. They could be open-ended but often have some sort of lens at the end. The world becomes your object chamber, since whatever the scope is pointed at becomes replicated. This is truly a different way of viewing the world.

The most basic chamber is fixed inside the last inch or so of the barrel. You view a scope with this type of object chamber by rotating the entire barrel. Another type of object chamber turns independently while the barrel is held in a fixed position. As the barrel or cell is turned, the objects tumble, and the image changes.

Yet another type of object chamber is the "wheel." Objects are incorporated into a relatively flat circle, usually larger than the barrel of the scope. The wheel is attached to the end of the barrel, and rotates independently. Naturally, wheels don't have to be flat. There are other quite fanciful shapes that are used as wheels. One very popular variation of the wheel (so popular, in fact, that it is generally given its own category) is the marble. A marble is attached to the end of the barrel, and is turned to produce different images. Some marbles are hand blown, some especially for kaleidoscopes. They can be quite dramatic, and are usually interchangeable. For interchangeable object chambers, wheels and marbles seem to be less complicated to engineer.

Interchangeable object chambers offer a lot of variety. With a single mirror system and presentation, the viewer gets multiple kaleidoscopes by changing the object chamber.

The objects in a chamber may be freely tumbling in air, or suspended in oil. An oil-filled chamber causes slower motion of the objects, and the motion continues after you have stopped rotating the scope.

Some object chambers are designed to be opened. Into these chambers, the viewer can insert different objects. These are quite effective for getting new views of common items.

When critiquing your object chamber, you will want to be sure that the turning is smooth, oil doesn't leak, and that all joinings are secure and appear "finished."

Objects

By now you know that objects can be contained within an object chamber or imbedded in a wheel. Objects considered most appropriate are colorful, small, textural, and translucent. These might be plastic or glass beads and chips, seeds, crystals, marbles, string...the list is endless. Textured, colorful glass is often used for wheels. Wildflowers and butterfly wings are examples of objects that are effective when cast in plastic wheels or sandwiched between clear panes. There are even scopes that use 35mm color slides as a wheel.

Messages, such as Happy Birthday, I Love You, and Get Well Soon, are sometimes used as objects. One of the most creative was a marriage proposal. You might think of coordinating a scope's message with its exterior to celebrate a special occasion.

Combining colors and shapes and sizes of objects is a personal and challenging process. It takes much experimentation to collect the objects that produce spectacular images. When I am looking at a scope, I am rarely aware of the particular pieces being used in the object chamber. What I do look for is constant surprise in the images, which, in general, means that the objects can move freely. I am wary of seemingly unintentional broken pieces, or pieces that stick in corners of the cell.

Variations

Some artists have mastered Brewster's polarized light scopes. Clear, flat objects are placed between polarized light filters for spectacular images with wonderful coloration. Sometimes the objects themselves are polarized. There are also scopes that use fluids of different colors. The colors don't mix with each other, and the replication of their swirling produces a delightful image. There is a sound-activated scope. A microphone in the circuitry activates the various shapes and colors. There are uses for fiber optics in scopes. A special variation is the projection scope. The images are rear-screen or forward-projected in varying sizes. (I am still waiting for a projection scope that I can afford.)

And for high-tech lovers, there is computer software that creates beautiful images. One program in the public domain is based on random generation, so the images are never repeated, and you can alter the speed at which the images change.

Other Considerations

In addition to the major components of exterior presentation, mirror system and object chamber, there are a few other factors to be aware of. The eyepiece, for example, is typically a round hole in a covering of the viewing end of the barrel. This hole is generally centered in respect to the mirror system. However, there are variations in shape, size and placement. The eyepiece may be a pointed oval or eye-shaped, or may be the full size and shape of the end of the mirror system. There are some binocular eyepieces. Some viewing holes are offset from the mirror system center, giving unusual views of the image.

To be sure your images are as clear as possible, you may want to use an optical lens in the eyepiece. Keeping in mind that the human eye (normal vision) has a minimum focal length of 6 to 8 inches, you may notice image distortion if your scope's length differs significantly. Optical lenses can also provide magnification of the image for even more impressive viewing. Lenses are either glass or plastic, and can be cut to fit your eyepiece. There are even collectors who have had special glasses or eyepiece attachments prepared for them to aid in viewing.

Another important consideration is the light source. Generally, you will have a transparent or translucent covering at the end of your object chamber, and the light will enter through that end of the scope. Some object chambers are designed to be side-lighted; that is, an opaque end piece is used for the object chamber, and the sides of the object chamber are translucent. Some kaleidoscopes are presented with internal light sources, or lights built into the stand of a parlor scope.

Whatever design technique you use, you must always be aware of how and where and how much light will enter your scope. After all, it is the reflection of light that produces an effective image.

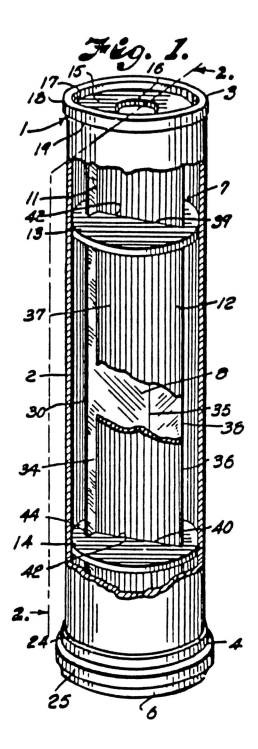

Fig. 1.

Drawing of kaleidoscope patented by H. B. Grow, 1961.

VIEWING

After investing the time to design and construct your kaleidoscope, you can spend the rest of your life enjoying it, and sharing it. Many kaleidoscope enthusiasts have had the experience of sharing a scope with someone who looks through it briefly, returns it, and says "you must see something in there that I don't." I think that must be true. Like most visual art, kaleidoscopic images are personal and interactive. The viewer brings his/her persona to the experience—and not everyone is willing or able to be so exposed.

There are different settings and techniques for enjoying your kaleidoscopes. While the usual technique is to aim the scope upward at a bright light, some scopes are more effective, or give a different experience, if viewed in the dark. You can use a lamp for a light source, but also try a focused beam from a small flashlight. Move the flashlight around to different angles and spots of light. Candlelight can also be an effective light source for some scopes. Effects produced with fluorescent and incandescent light are also interesting. Of course, many scopes are particularly dramatic in bright sunlight. Also, simply tapping the barrel is sometimes more effective than rotating it. Varying the speed at which you turn the object chamber produces different viewing experiences. In fact, some members of the kaleido-community are known as either "fast turners" or "slow turners."

Kaleidoscopic viewing makes great party entertainment. One couple who received a scope for a wedding gift reportedly had to remind guests that they were there to visit, not to look at scopes. It is certainly fun to "ooh and aah," and try to pass an especially wonderful image intact to a friend. On the other hand, solitary viewing offers a rich, internally satisfying experience.

It seems that I am able to get whatever I need at the moment from a viewing experience. It is the nature of a scope that it can be either stimulating or soothing. By focusing on the intricacies of the pattern, I feel excitement. Or by concentrating on the totality, the symmetry, I feel calmed.

To enable myself to explore creative solutions to vocational or personal problems, I use kaleidoscope viewing to keep my mind open, to look for different alternatives. Many professional people report keeping a few scopes in the office for just that exercise. I also find that kaleidoscope viewing is a healthy way of relaxing and coping with stress. I see beauty and wholeness, and a reminder that there is harmony in all of life's changes.

Therapists are using the kaleidoscope as a metaphor to help clients understand life cycles. They are also recommended for helping in the search for balance of body, mind and spirit. Health organizations have found kaleidoscopes helpful in accomplishing some of their goals. The Hospice organization has used scopes with both dying patients and family members. Children's hospitals use scopes with patients undergoing long treatment. Holding and turning scopes and getting such immediate reward in beautiful images is also good therapy for people who need to exercise their hands. Kaleidoscopes are particularly effective in enhancing meditation. It seems to me that all kaleidoscope viewing is a form of meditation, even unconsciously. Perhaps it is a joyful and fun experience, but at the same time we are gaining a renewal of spirit. We get the benefit of color and harmony in every viewing, whether it is purposeful concentration or not.

While I participated for years in what I skeptically called "recreational growth experiences," I could not understand the talk about "centering" yourself. I had no idea what this meant, and had no clue how to accomplish it. Finally, viewing a mandala image, I could understand. Over time I have been able to internalize the balance, harmony, and wholeness of the images into my own mind and spirit. This didn't happen immediately. For the first year or so, I just knew that I found scopes relaxing and peaceful, and better than a glass of wine for getting to sleep at night. I even felt an unexplained and warm kinship with the scope artists and collectors that I met. Now I have come to feel there must be some exchange of "soul" that occurs when I view a scope, even by an artist I have never met.

So as you are creating your kaleidoscopes, and putting some of your soul into them, know that you are communicating with those who will view your scopes. They may appreciate your craftsmanship, but in seeing the images you've created, they may also glimpse the beauty in your soul. This is truly a wonderful gift.

Dan Sudnick

This one-of-a-kind kaleidoscope, entitled "Vocation-Avocation," is a combination of my vocational skills as a plumber and the reflection of my mind's eye. It began 20 years ago as a project at a trade school open-house to demonstrate the joining of copper pipe and fittings, and has continued to evolve. I admit that it may never be finished, as I continue to add old or unusual fittings from time to time. My interest in kaleidoscopes was inspired by my wife, a very creative mechanical engineer. She started making kaleidoscopes from stained glass years ago.

The lamp-scope shown here has three kaleidoscopes mounted in various positions. Each scope can be removed for individual viewing. One scope has an object case filled with oil. The second scope has three hand-blown glass marbles, and the third scope has four interchangeable object cases. Each object case or marble is displayed in a unique fashion under each scope. I have since created another series of intricate plumbing scopes entitled "Copper Madness."

"Vocation-Avocation" lamp stand incorporates five handmade scopes, each with interchangeable marbles and object chambers.

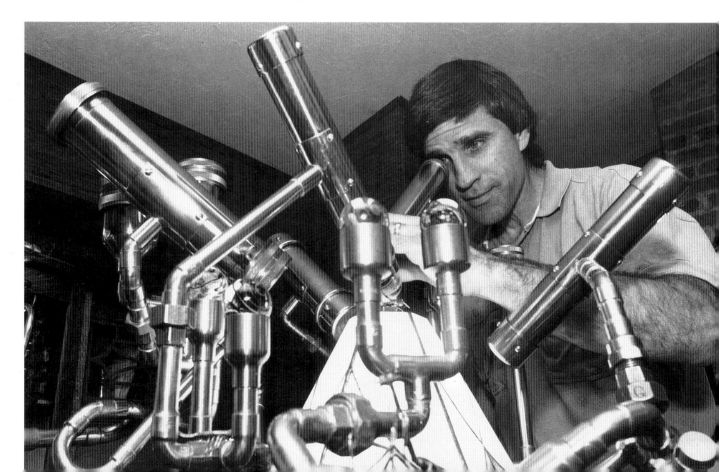

Willie Stevenson

"Outbound: An In-Viro-Mental Statement" (above).

"Home Planet #1" (below).

My approach to making scopes is that of a sculptor, creating signed and numbered limited editions, of which "Home Planet #1" and "Outbound: An In-Viro-Mental Statement" (a 1991 Niche Award winner) are examples. I also do one-of-a-kinds and am available for commissioned work with special emphasis on coin operation and kinetics.

My most notable piece to date is a winner of the Brewster Society Award For Creative Ingenuity titled "Whatever Blows Your Skirt Up," now residing in the home/museum of Cozy Baker and renamed by her, "Whatever Tilts Your Kilts." It's a 6' L. x 6' H. x 3' W., motorized, poly-angular scope with hand-painted silks revolving above a fan at the object-end of the 12" x 48" first surface mirrors. Stereo speakers at the eyepiece provide continuous music. At the flip of the switch the mirrors start opening and closing, and the stunning, randomly formed image dances seductively in perfect beat to whatever music is playing. The matching of the audio and visual elements is what I call "cerebrally synchro-nized," and the total experi-ence is a kaleidoscopic mas-sage for the soul.

Steven Gray

As of late, kaleidoscopes have offered a wonderful mixture of optics, woodwork, gadgetry and a freedom of design which fits my personality very well. Kaleidoscopes have such a fascination and mystique that to do them justice, I feel that the outside appearance should have an attraction making it hard for most people to pass them by without stopping to investigate further. Although kaleidoscopes go back to the early 1800s, there are no prescribed limits on artistic interpreta-

Interior view of parasol pattern (left).

tions. My current designs have no traditional counterparts, although my interpretation might remind one of old world navigating devices.

Another important aspect to me is the selection of wood and the effect that it will have on the overall feeling of the kaleidoscope. Since I use some exceptionally figured woods, it is very important that I use the wood to its fullest potential. Only then have I done the wood justice. My reward is the satisfaction and enjoyment of a wonderful piece of wood fashioned into an object of an equally pleasing nature.

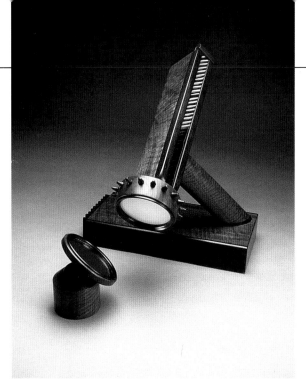

Stephen and Carmen Gallo Colley

"Silver Diner," an Ultra model, is a multi-media scope with blinking light emitting diode.

"Garden of Eden," detail (bottom).

In 1978, we were stained glass panel designers and joined an artist co-op gallery in downtown San Antonio. Most customers were tourists looking for small gifts which travel well in suitcases. Producing such an item was the inspiration for the first Gallocolley kaleidoscope.

Thirteen years and hundreds of kaleidoscopes later, the table top and jewelry kaleidoscopes we produce bear little resemblance to our first ones. Working on the theory that there is no such thing as too much embellishment, and driven by the feeling that each scope should look better than the one made before it, Gallocolley Opdesign table scopes include just about any kind of material which can withstand the heat of assembly. The Ultra model scopes, each with a unique name, design and theme, can include as many as 400 individual parts and often take over 120 hours to produce.

Carmen relies on her jewelry construction background to make her necklace scopes. These tiny scopes incorporate precious and semi-precious jewels, stones and heat-treated glass particles to provide an easy way to take the colorful and soothing kaleidoscopic images everywhere.

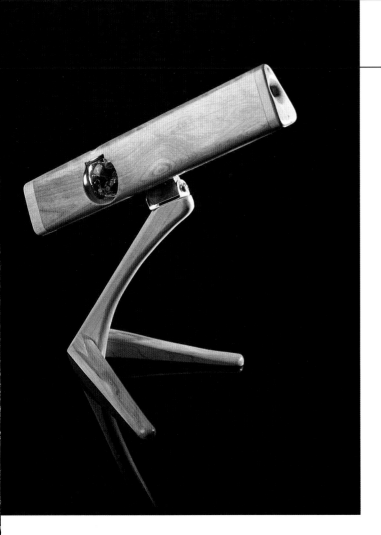

Henry Bergeson

I started out as a mechanical engineer working on projects ranging from the development of modern sailing rigs for cargo ships, to boat building and medical instrument design. While certain aspects of this work were always interesting, I felt there was something lacking in terms of creative freedom. When a downturn in business found me out of a job, I had some freedom to explore other directions. That freedom led to a happy entanglement in the world of kaleidoscopes. My focus in this world has been to gather up bits of my past experiences and knowledge to create unique, interactive kaleidoscopes with extraordinary images and rugged construction.

"Luna Scope" (left) is a 2-mirror parlor scope that is detachable. It features a hand-blown glass object chamber with its own rechargeable light source. "Treasure Chest" (below) is a versatile scope available in 2- or 3-mirror format with interchangeable objects. Photos by Michael Fulks.

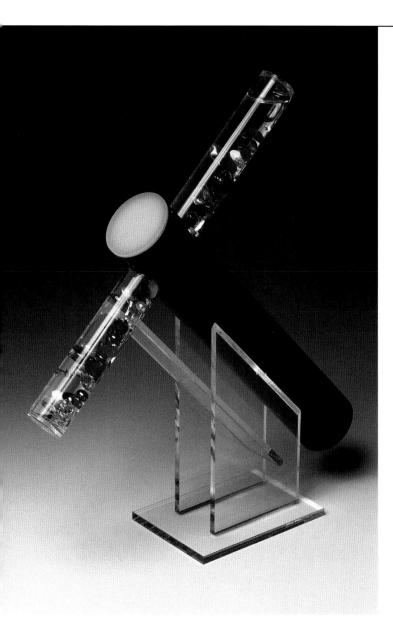

David Kalish

The kaleidoscope is a wonderful optical instrument that creates order out of chaos, providing us with a sense of symmetry, balance, and harmony. These are elements which I attempt to carry over into the exterior designs of each of my works.

Special emphasis is given to the interior optical components of my kaleidoscopes. The object cases contain pieces suspended in pure mineral oil. Mostly natural objects are used. Pieces are carefully selected and combined to produce optimum imaging. Lighting is an essential ingredient. My designs utilize variable front and side lighting with different backgrounds and translucencies.

"Melting Moments" (above) features an unusual oil-filled object chamber. Photo by Douglas Campbell.

My wood pieces have been created in collaboration with fellow craftsman Thomas Crothers. We use a variety of exotic hardwoods. The brass pieces are made of solid brass, buffed to a mirror finish.

My creations are both sculptural and architectural with a distinctively modern, contemporary look.

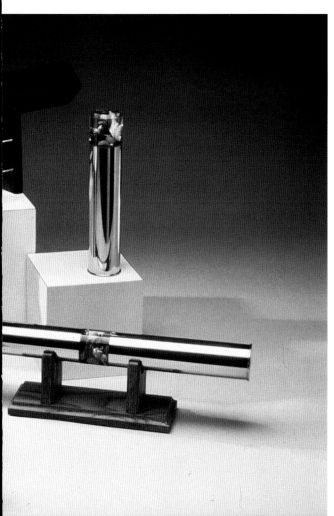

Interior (top), photo by Douglas Campbell.

An array of designs (left) including, clockwise from left: "Odyssey," "Sea Fantasy - I," "The Wedding - I," "Sea Fantasy - II," "The Wedding - II," and "Classical Brass." Photo by Ron Didinato.

Dean Krause

When I was about eight years old, I dismantled my first kaleidoscope. Twenty-one years later I built my first, for a friend. Eventually, I began selling them, and giving them as gifts. Kaleidoscopes are, to me, a very unique art form. Part machine, part divine, they unite the human qualities that are usually separate. They illustrate that order can come out of chaos. The viewer has a sense of involvement, being able to change their view of the world at will.

I have many reasons to build kaleidoscopes, but by far, expressing my own creativity is the most important. I feel that artists change the state of consciousness they

experience, then create something that has that energy ingrained into it. If others are open to the experience, they can use that art as a bridge, to become a different person.

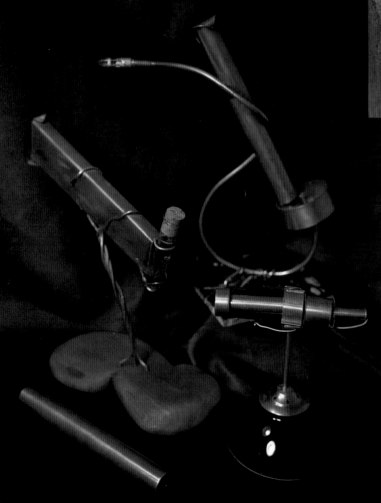

"Kaleido-Ring," top, and "Beautiful," bottom (photo above) feature dichroic glass objects with 2-mirror systems. Photo by Mark Wenzel.

Four scopes (left), clockwise from front left: Kaleido-8"; "Pillars of the Universe," an organic parlor scope with 4-mirror system; "Uxmal," with turning quartz crystal and green marble slab; "Captain Nemo's Personal Ray Machine," a battery-powered kaleido projector with changeable object cells. Photo by Eric Lovejoy.

Audrey Barna

When I was a child, my father raised poultry. My mother once attended a lecture on egg art, where it was mentioned that goose eggs were very much in demand among egg artists. Through this contact, I met someone who introduced me to the world of egging.

I believe I am the first person to make a kaleidoscope egg. I wanted to make something different, something I had never seen done before with an egg. I had always loved kaleidoscopes, but don't know exactly what triggered the connection.

Egg art has been the most fulfilling thing I have ever done in my life. It provides an income, friends, travel, business experience, an outlet for creativity, respect of my peers, and self esteem. Also, the geese, ducks and chickens are earning their keep!

Goose egg scopes with front-turning 2-mirror systems. Photo by Tess Scherer.

33

Charles Karadimos

As a self-taught glass artist since 1976 and kaleidoscope maker since 1979, dealing with light and color have been a primary concern. The kaleidoscope fulfills this, not just because it is a colorful toy, but because it enables one to respond immediately to various combinations of color, shape, and light with the simple turning of an object case.

All of my scopes are handcrafted entirely of glass, with individuality and quality being of utmost importance. The exteriors are constructed using fusing and slumping techniques, with the focus on a clean look and a balanced feel. However, the imagery produced by the scope I feel is the most important aspect. All of the glass in the free-moving object case is selected to

coordinate with the exterior glass. Since it is imperative that color balance and random imagery be maintained, each piece is carefully shaped, lamp-worked, melted, fused, and/or cut. This, in combination with a variety of mirror systems, results in patterns that are very intricate, attention-holding and emotion-provoking.

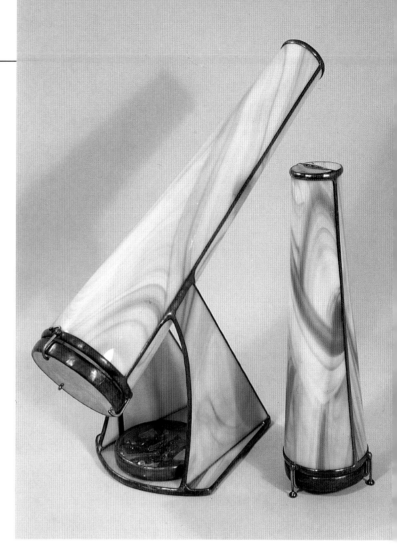

"Obelisk," with battery-powered interior lights (opposite top).

"Fused/Slumped Set" with inter-changeable object cases (opposite bottom).

Interior image with six-point symmetry (top left).

"Cone" and "Parlor Cone," made of slumped glass (top right).

"Delta II" binocular, with 3-D image (left).

35

Douglas Johnson

The new kaleidoscope designs I have created (marble scope, satellite scopes, scopeitall, binocular scope and the carousel) have emerged because of a playful attitude, a willingness to explore, and a fascination with the questions, "I wonder how it will look if…" and "How can the kaleidoscope experience be improved?"

As one of the early pioneers of this particular kaleidoscope renaissance, I emerged through the stained glass world. Windseye kaleidoscopes reflect this origin as well as an earlier fascination with 19th century brass instrument technology. My work has been described by others as typifying the "Jules Verne" era.

Kaleidoscopes have been for me the greatest possible playground of opportunities! Through kaleidoscopic creation, invention, design, and production I have been able to realize almost all of my childhood and adult dreams.

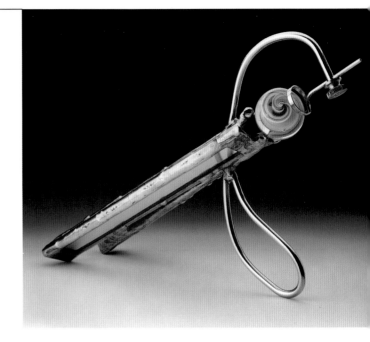

"Windseye Marble Binocular Kaleidoscope" (above). Photo by Chuck Johnson.

"Carousel," "Light Vein," "Crystoscope," and "Rolascope," from top (below). Photo by Ralph Grabriner.

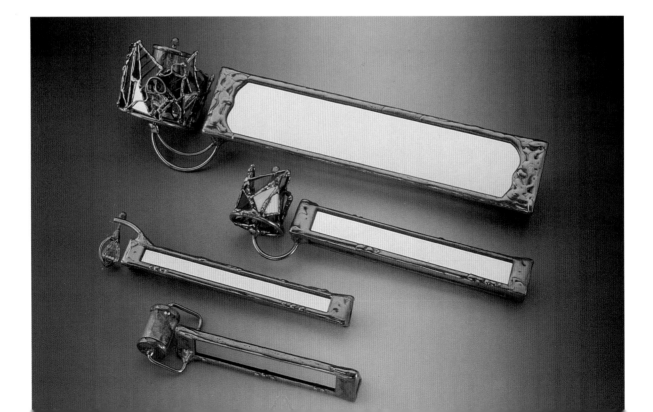

Don Doak

When making a kaleidoscope, my goal is to create a quality scope that, 100 years from today, an antique collector will be able to spot from across the room and immediately identify as a "Don Doak kaleidoscope." By applying all the skills, crafts, and trades I have worked at in my life, I feel I may be able to achieve this goal.

I design and build many of my tools, ranging from a special glass cutter to cut my mirror, to building a large kiln capable of rapidly bending, fusing and/or irridizing glass in an airtight, controlled environment.

Each kaleidoscope is made completely by me. My scopes are labor-intensive, and the design I have developed is unique, as it came from within me. From the beginning, I have felt that, rather than coming up with a new design every few months, I would strive to improve and perfect the design I have. My hope is that by combining precision in shape, form, function, quality material and workmanship, I will someday produce the perfect kaleidoscope.

Two "Liquid Wheel" kaleidoscopes (below) with two "Musical Geodyssey" scopes and accessory box, all made of irridized glass. Photo by Schepp.

David and Marty Roenigk

Sir David's Reflections was started by brothers David and Marty Roenigk due to the demand for antique kaleidoscopes. We started out by collecting antique scopes and selling extras. When the demand got too great, we decided to produce exact reproductions using the same materials, paying particular attention to size, weight and mirror systems. But because we believe that the objects in the object case are the heart and soul of the kaleidoscope, we faithfully reproduced the same glass and designs that the original artists intended for each scope. We also employed Steve Auger to design new objects for a new look in the old scopes.

"The Queen Anne" (above) features a changeable object case and collapses to 3 inches.

Object case (right) from **"The Victoria II."**

"The Victoria II" (opposite) is a brass and mahogany parlorscope containing precious and semi-precious stones as well as detailed lampwork ampules in its object case.

Shantidevi

My work, life work, art work, inner and outer work is about healing. It's about bringing some light, laughter and natural order into a world that has lost its connection to a natural sense of the divine. Kaleidoscopes have always been a mystical vehicle for me. The ever changing gifts within transport me to that place in the heart of silence that nourishes my spirit and sustains my courage in these tumultuous times. The spheres I've made are also spiritual for me. Even their form is synonymous with wholeness. I experience a deep peacefulness holding and viewing them. It is my hope that my work will move others for a moment to that place that is bigger than all of us and contains all of our differences in grace and beauty, a reminder of our unity with all.

Group of kaleidoscopes and spheres (above).

"Let the Dreamers Wake the Nation" (right), by Shantidevi and Sugito, with spheres and object chamber containing liquid filled ampules.

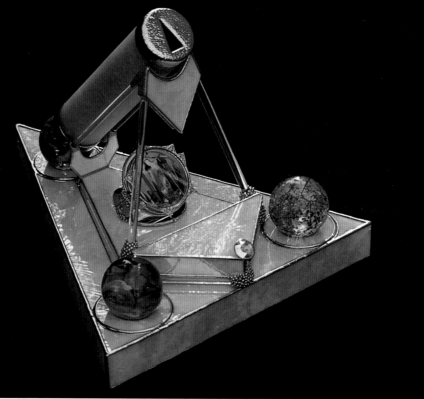

Dorothy Marshall

When I made my first kaleidoscope in 1971, I didn't realize I would be poor as a churchmouse and living in an unheated attic while I struggled to break through the prevailing notion of kaleidoscopes as "just a dimestore toy." After hundreds of discouraging rejections from fair directors and gallery owners, perseverance paid off and my handmade kaleidoscopes were accepted into the top arts and crafts shows in the country where they won various awards. Favorable reviews in the New York Times and other media followed.

Luckily, about this time I fell in love with Ethan Allen, a scientist. Together we drafted a proposal for an exhibit which integrated the art and science of kaleidoscopes. I became the creative director of this exhibit, *Kaleidoscopes: Reflections of Science and Art,* which was toured nationally for three years by the Smithsonian with primary funding from the National Science Foundation. It firmly established kaleidoscopes' newly won credibility with millions of museum visitors. At Harvard, other universities, and the

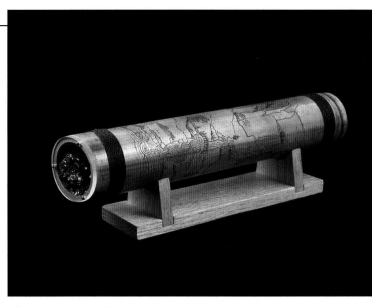

"Chinese Landscape" by Dorothy Marshall and Indra Stern, made of flame-tempered handcarved bamboo. Photo by Carol Westlake.

Smithsonian, our classes sold out and received rave reviews.

Ethan and I also developed a Kaleido-Kit which is environmentally friendly, guaranteed, educationally powerful, and maintains the highest standards for optical quality and user safety.

Scott Cole

I have been developing the use of a variety of styles and materials in making kaleidoscopes since 1982. Specializing in custom scopes, I am a pioneer in the artistic use of blown glass and anodized aluminum bodies.

With a background in teaching, I enjoy sharing my enthusiasm and expertise by conducting kaleidoscope workshops. I am also a counselor by profession, and continue to explore the connections between creativity and personal growth.

Two scopes made with anodized aluminum encased in blown glass.

41

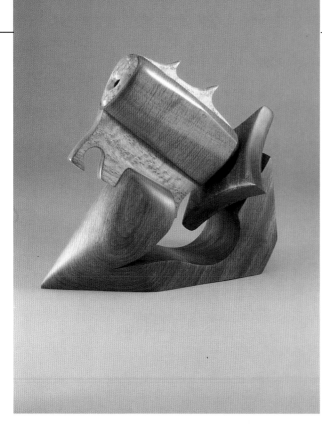

Carol Paretti

Kaleidoscopes are an exciting art form because they allow the artist to explore many different media while also investigating the technical aspects of the kaleidoscopic image.

Kaleidoscopes have magical, kinetic and sensory qualities to them. The exterior of the kaleidoscope can be something beautiful to look at, touch, and in the case of our aromatic cedar scopes, even smell. Then, while looking through a small aperature, you are able to enjoy a larger magical world of constantly changing color and form.

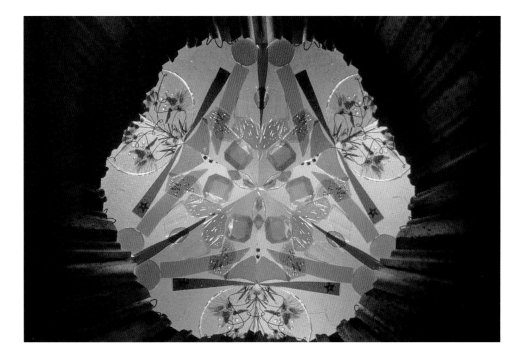

"Angler" (opposite top), "Whimsy" (opposite bottom), and "Series 640 Variation" (below), each made of exotic woods, with 2-mirror systems, fluted wood interiors and interchangeable object chambers. Photos by Terry Pemberton.

Alfred Brickel

Art is not held at arms' length. Art is inter-reactive—artist with medium—the discovery of a bright spirit within us, from child up.

The world's largest kaleidoscope. (Interior view, below)

Amy Hnatko

Because kaleidoscopes spend most of the time on tables or shelves, I wanted to create pieces that would be as beautiful to look at as to look through. When I began to make kaleidoscopes, there were few articles or books on the subject, so I had to solve the technical problems as well as the aesthetic ones. This led to many mistakes, but also to solutions which were uniquely my own. I tend to think three-dimensionally, and my designs often seem to spring into my mind in surprisingly complete detail. My many years spent working in stained glass gives me the experience to solve the structural problems. At some point during the construction, I have to let go of the initial idea and allow the piece to find its own form. My reward comes when my new design is finally completed—if it comes close to satisfying my original idea.

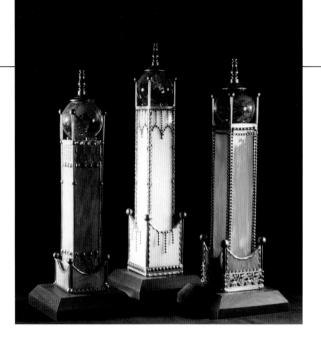

"Chinese Dragon" (below). Photo by Henry Tenbroeke.

"Xanadu Series" (above), with hand blown globes by Donna Fein. Photo by Amy Hnatko.

"Northern Lights" (opposite), with hand blown globe by Donna Fein. Photo by Henry Tenbroeke.

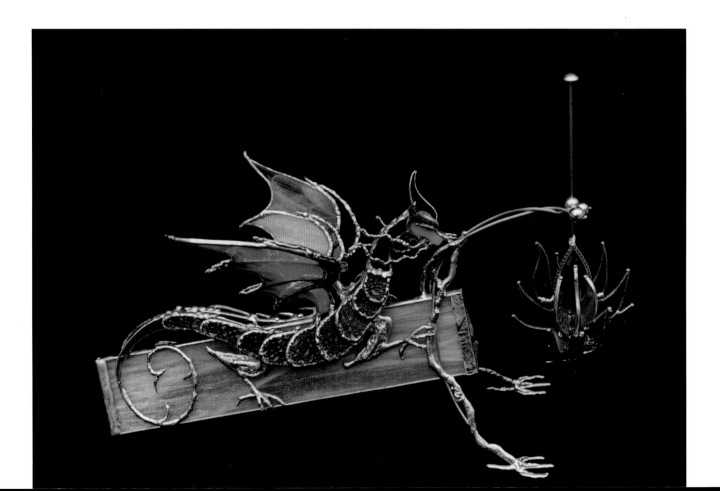

Sam Douglas

Kaleidoscopes offer me a synthesis of a lifetime's interests, experiences, techniques and abilities. This unique blend of instrument, toy and potential artwork—and the necessity for a kaleidoscope to fulfill a variety of roles—is challenging both technically and artistically.

No kaleidoscope is ever the same; no image repeats itself. Each work is both micro- and macro-cosm; it establishes its own ecology. That's why I call them Kaleidescapes, which combines the notion of "escape" with the ever-changing geography of a new landscape—an infinite journey in an eight-inch mirror. A twist of the wrist can alter the image utterly. The viewer of the scope becomes a collaborator, an image-maker as well.

My signature Kaleidescapes—the Empire State or Chrysler Building—contain a strange magic. It's a special moment to present such a piece and hear an adult laugh with a child's spontaneous delight at the mere sight of it…laugh at the idea of a secret world waiting inside a familiar form.

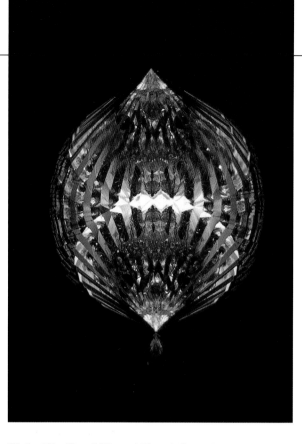

"Solar Wind" and "Crystal Phoenix" acrylic scopes (below), with interior images produced by Solar Wind (above) and Magna Sphere (opposite). Photos by Lawrence Tagrin.

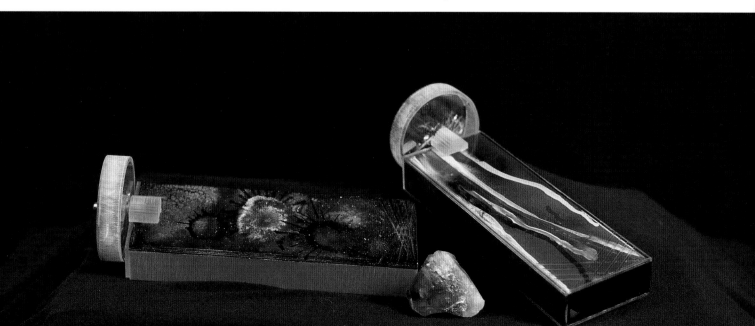

Randy & Shelley Knapp

We believe we do more than produce kaleidoscopes; we give them life. By combining our talents in design, woodworking and sculpting, we create scopes that burst on the consciousness with color and light.

After settling our debts and quitting our jobs, we've devoted our energies to developing this art form. Our backgrounds in cabinetmaking, glazing, glass blowing, and even quiltmaking, have enabled us to produce unique scopes of the highest quality. We are always looking for new ways to utilize our technical skills and to put our heart and soul into each new design, which hopefully will endure through many generations.

Interior image from "Twilight" (above).

"Twilight" (opposite top) features a unique side light object chamber containing flame sculpted dichroic glass and "stringerinis."

"Fly By" (opposite bottom) pivots in any position and can be detached from the base. Among the objects in its chamber are liquid filled ampules by the Falconers.

"Verticulation" (above) contains 60 pieces of hand blown glass suspended in fluid to rotate vertically.

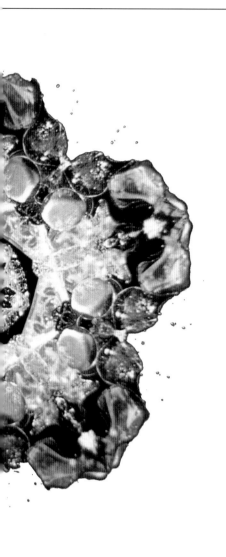

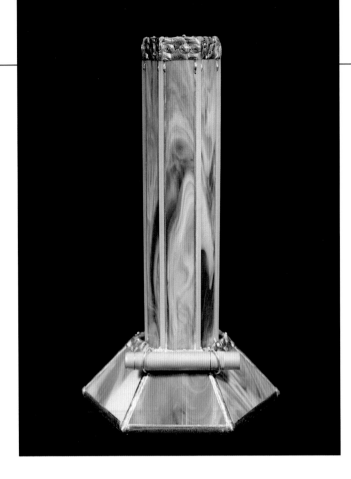

Sherry Moser

As a child growing up with a father who was a watercolor artist, color always held great fascination for me. I remember sitting beside him as he painted. It seems only natural that this color interest included the sparkling, changing images of toy kaleidoscopes.

As an adult, stained glass work is a stress-relieving hobby for my nursing profession. Stained glass rekindled my interest in color. Several years ago, I also discovered the wonderful world of contemporary kaleidoscopes. I put my glass skills to work and began creating my own kaleido-scopes.

The mandala images created by my pieces have special meaning for me. Mandalas have been used throughout history to promote balance, unity and healing, while also depicting the cyclic nature of life.

"Light Dancer" (opposite, top) on its base, with pen light viewing accessory.

Interior view of "Chandala" scope (opposite, bottom), with its 3-D dichroic effect.

"The Journey," with exterior and interior views. Photos by David Moser.

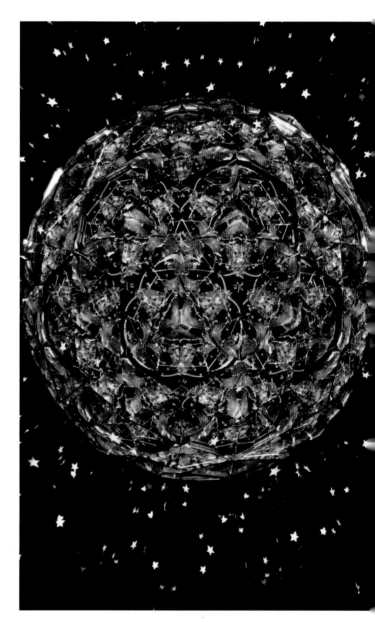

Dennis & Diane Falconer

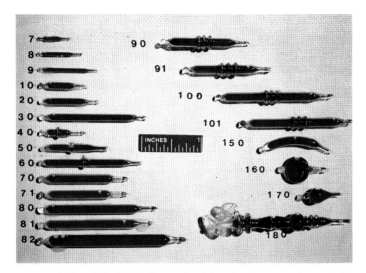

Styles of liquid filled ampules (above); colors are also varied.

"Ice Cave" (below) is made of handblown Pyrex glass and contains liquid filled ampules in a rotating, oil filled object chamber.

Our interest in kaleidoscopes developed over the years that we were collecting them. That interest turned to a love of the art form when I decided to make Diane an all handblown glass kaleidoscope, with liquid filled ampules, for our collection. It took my 25 years of experience as a scientific glassblower to accomplish this task. "Ice Cave" was truly a labor of love.

Since the limited edition "Ice Cave" we have developed other collector scopes. For these scopes, we chose to merge metal and wood together in our Fire Series. The fire refers to the polarized images. The colors correspond to the color of the exterior of each scope.

We spent a year developing and designing an array of multi-color filled ampules that are among the smallest ever created. As our scope designs unfold, these colorful components should enhance the value of our scopes.

Skeeter & Pete De Mattia

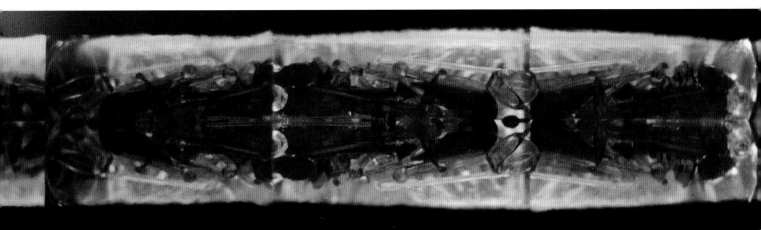

We are a husband and wife team, working out of the basement of our home. Five years ago we began collecting kaleidoscopes. Pete has had several vocations. He left his last job to devote full time to kaleidoscope making. Most recently he has been excited by a newly developed camera small enough to capture the interior of almost any kaleidoscope.

Necklaces were first. A glass tube acts as the reflective surface of the single dichroic wheel. Swirls of brilliant blues, pinks, and golds whirl before your eyes. Discovering irridized glass, we added a second wheel, which adds purples and greens to the images and alters the hues of the existing colors for a wondrous array of color. Color manipulation is the key to this scope. By rotating the wheels slowly, you can paint a palette of spiraling color.

From our excitement emerged the Warp Factor Series. Each scope in this series has a truncated, triangular shaped body. Warp Factor One is the first one-mirror scope known in existence. In Warp Factor Five, a unique vastness of space and light prevails, where columns arise, and "roads of light and color" come at you and recede into the distance.

Our most current design is the Warp Factor Two plus One, having a large spherical image with partial reflections adjacent to it. Ranking among the newer artists, we have a lifetime of ideas waiting to be made.

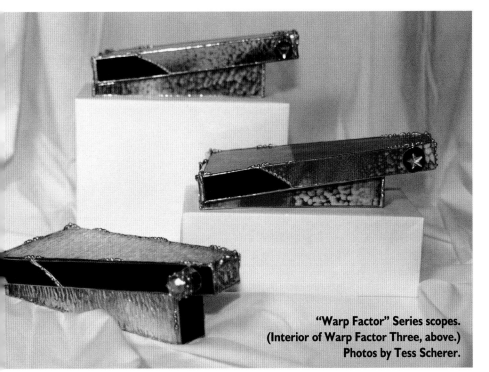

**"Warp Factor" Series scopes.
(Interior of Warp Factor Three, above.)
Photos by Tess Scherer.**

55

THE PRINCIPLES OF DESIGN

While kaleidoscopes may vary greatly in appearance and quality, there are four primary elements in any design:

1. the eye piece
2. the body
3. the mirror system
4. the object chamber

Each of these elements has its own set of variables, involving design configurations, dimensions, choice of materials, and construction techniques. Each combination of design elements produces its own unique image, which, in turn, produces endless variations from the objects being viewed.

The Eye Piece

The eye piece opening usually conforms to the shape of the mirror system in some way. It may open to the full viewing area, shrink toward the center or to one side, be shaped by external style considerations, be binocular, or even multiple if more than one mirror system is housed in the body. When designing your own scope, view the image through your prototype to best determine the appropriate placement, size and shape of the opening.

The other eyepiece consideration is the lens. You may choose to leave your eyepiece open, but be careful that the scope is handled most carefully so that loosened objects from the chamber or tiny chips of glass from the mirrors do not fall into your eye as you tilt it up for viewing. You may elect to cut a glass eyepiece, but again watch for breakage. The best option is plastic. Depending on your focal length, you may need an optical lens for magnification—either for tiny scopes or for visual effect. If your focal length is less than about 7 inches, you should use a lens for the specific distance between the eyepiece and the object chamber.

The Body

The kaleidoscope body merely houses the optical system, yet it should be regarded as the major external element in terms of visual presentation. The options are endless: round or faceted cylinders, tapered cylinders, flared or curved, and composed of any conceivable materials and added ornamentation. Another design consideration to be integrated with the construction of the body is the possible need for a stand or mount. If your scope is not free-standing (or lying), you may want to construct a cradle holder of similar material. Some bodies may incorporate legs of some kind to support them. A typical parlor-scope would be affixed to a stand at an angle, which might be adjustable. More elaborate mounts could involve belt-cranks or worm and tooth gears to either rotate the objects in the chamber or the angles of an adjustable mirror system.

The usual materials and construction techniques for creating kaleidoscope bodies are shown in the projects in this book: cardboard, plastics, metal, wood, and stained glass. Other possibilities include ceramic, fabric, blown glass, or any other material that can be fashioned into a rigid structure. The ornamentation of these surfaces can involve: various painting techniques (spraying, paper wrapping, marbleizing, stenciling, spinning, drip and splatter), gluing, soldering, etching, staining, inlay, glazing, sewing, etc.

The Mirror System

Mirror systems entail choice of material, dimension, angles and configuration. They are the soul of the kaleidoscope. You can experiment with acetate, metals, foil and mylar, especially if you are creating a cylindrical, spiral, or convex mirror system. Otherwise, you ought to consider 2nd or 1st surface mirrors. For optical quality, 1st surface mirrors are worth the extra investment. The overall size of your system may also be a factor.

The more crucial component for image production is mirror configuration. Two- and three-mirror systems are the most popular. Both are configured as a triangular cylinder, housed in some sort of tube.

The two-mirror system is shaped like a "V," with a 3rd side across the top that is blackened. The angle of the "V" determines the pattern of replication, as follows:

90°	-	4 images,	2 point star
60 °	-	6 images,	3 point star
45°	-	8 images,	4 point star
36°	-	10 images,	5 point star
30°	-	12 images,	6 point star
25.7°	-	14 images,	7 point star
22.5°	-	16 images,	8 point star
20°	-	18 images,	9 point star
18°	-	20 images,	10 point star
16.8°	-	22 images,	11 point star
15°	-	24 images,	12 point star

Three-mirror systems can be arranged in any form of triangle, and produce a continuous field of honeycomb-like patterns, so long as the sum of the three angles equals 180°. Here are three common patterns:

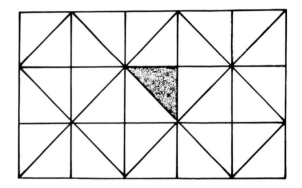

45° - 45° - 90°

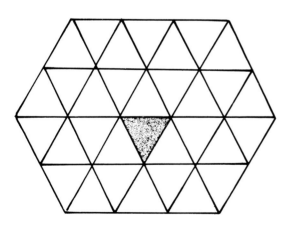

60° - 60° - 60°

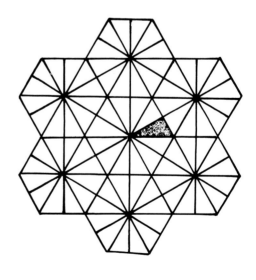

30° - 60° - 90°

Square, rectangular, and larger multiples produce images reflective of each shape. Tapered mirrors of three or more sides produce an interesting spherical image:

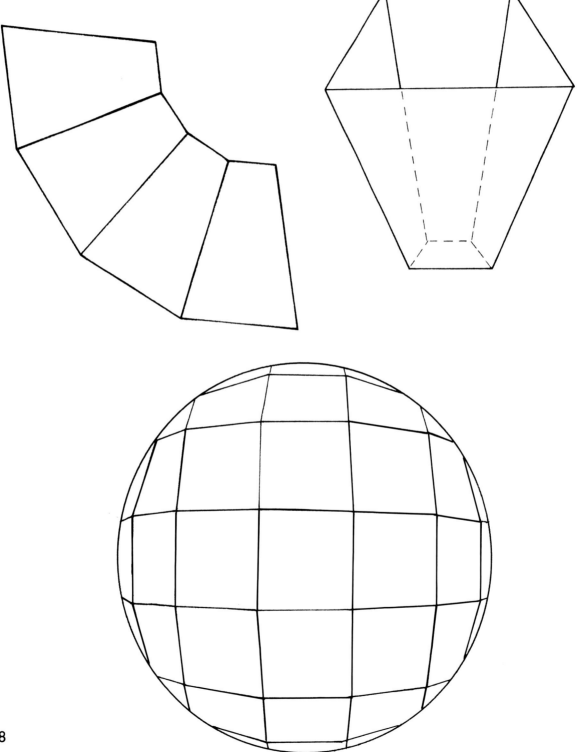

Cylindrical and spiral reflective surfaces will create images that reach through the barrel asymmetrically. Another option is to incorporate an apparatus for adjusting the angle of the mirrors (usually two) to achieve a range of image capability. It is also possible to contain two separate mirror systems within the body of the scope, each with its own eyepiece and viewpoint of the object chamber. Binocular systems have also been developed.

Mirrors can be mounted inside the body using any number of materials: foamcore, styrofoam, wooden strips, thick cloth; or they may be fit so exactly that a few spots of glue will suffice. The most common and effective way to join the mirror system is with duct tape.

The Object Chamber

If your scope is to be a teleidoscope, there will not be an object chamber, unless optionally attached for kaleidoscopic viewing. However, a teleidoscope can utilize lenses tht filter the light, such as with tinted, textured or faceted glass. Some chambers may be designed to be opened, for changing the objects inside. Others may be fixed to the body, so that the objects tumble as the whole body is turned. Still others have object chambers that rotate independently of the body, either in line or on a perpendicular axis. They may be detachable, interchangeable, containing colored fluids, or various add-on features.

The objects within the chamber are open to the imagination, yet are often coordinated with the exterior presentation of the scope in terms of color and texture. They may be composed of recognizable subject matter, abstract objects, or other fluid forms. They may be chosen for their color, shape, texture, weight, transparency, translucency, or opacity. There are alternative

formats, such as frames for 35 mm slides, drum and strip panoramas, and hand-drawn images as viewing objects.

With lighting properties and size as criteria, here are some possible objects for chambers:

broken colored glass and plastic

melted glass and plastic

broken auto windshields

mirror fragments

translucent stones and crystals

small polished stones

small colored beads

faceted and colored beads

tiny colored rods

small trinkets

small opaque objects

paperclips and metal fragments

various seashells

laminated flower petals, insect wings

marbles and ball bearings

sequins, glitter and stars

cellophane scraps

acetates: colored, frosted, scored

Having designed and composed the object chamber, there is the consideration of lighting. Mostly, your source will be natural light, but you may want the option of an artificial light source incorporated into your design—either fixed or moveable. Generally, light can be directed from the front and/or the side of the object chamber. It may also be diffused through a translucent pane, focused or bent through a lens, or filtered through tinted, textured, polarized, or dichroic glass.

Basic Construction Techniques

Cutting Glass

This technique may seem a bit formidable to the novice, but can be mastered fairly easily with a little practice. You will need a glass cutter, a black felt-tip pen, a straight edge ruler, and some glass scraps to practice a few cuts.

First, measure and draw the exact shape onto the glass with the pen and the ruler, with lines extending fully to all edges. Place the glass on a table in front of you. Hold the glass cutter with the fingertips of both hands, lay the wheel on the far end of one of your longer marks, and draw it straight toward you down the mark until it rolls off the near edge (see Photo 1). The motion should be smooth and continuous with moderate, even pressure. You must score the glass only once for each cut. Keeping the wheel of your cutter oiled will prolong its life.

Once the glass is scored, grasp the near edge with thumbs over fists either side of the scored line, yet close together (see Photo 2). Rotate fists

firmly, with thumbs turning out from each other, pushing up from underneath to snap the glass apart and down the cut in one motion. Do not coax this process by first tapping under the scored cut with the ball end of the cutter, as other glass cutters do. This creates uneven edges unsuitable for mirror seams or stained glass joints. When cutting stained or textured glass, always score the smooth side. Also, be sure to wear safety goggles when cutting glass.

Cutting gentle curves utilizes this same technique. Severe and multiple curves are more difficult. To cut a disc, score and break a series of lines (as shown in the drawing), then even up the edge by chipping off irregularities with the notches in your glass cutter (see Photo 3).

Photo 2

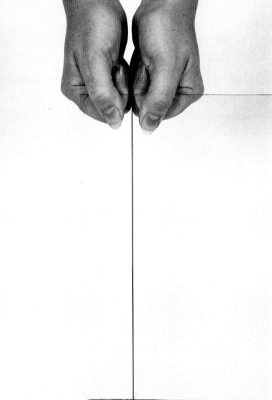

Photo 1

60

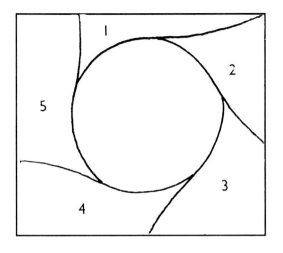

Since this is somewhat difficult, it is preferable to cut a disc from plexiglas using a fine tooth coping saw. Leave the adhesive backing on both sides until the cut is made. Edges can be smoothed, if necessary, with a file.

Joining Stained Glass

Your local stained glass or hobby shop can supply you with tools and materials for this operation. Having cut all your glass pieces, you should clean them with window cleaner or grease-cutting dishwashing liquid. Do be careful of sharp edges. Once thoroughly dried, wrap all the edges with copper foil (see Photo 4). Peel away a length of the adhesive backing, center the foil on an edge, press it and continue working your way around the perimeter, finishing with an overlap of about 1/4 inch. Then crimp the edges around both surfaces, making sure the foil adheres securely.

Practice the soldering technique on some scrap, to get the feel of it. First, using a flux

Photo 4

brush, apply "paste flux" to all surfaces of the copper foil. Then, place the tip of your soldering iron to the foil and touch the tip of some 50-50 solid core wire solder next to it until it flows over the foil (see Photo 5). Continue applying a thin coat of solder over the foil in a continuous motion around the edges until they are covered.

When all your pieces have been coated in

Photo 3

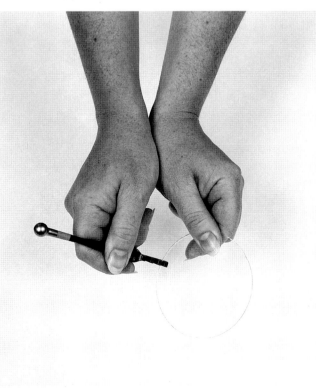

61

Photo 5

Photo 6

this way, you can assemble all or part of your structure using masking tape. Then, at the corners or other critical junctures, tack solder those spots by placing the tip of your iron on both edges to be joined, and touch your wire solder to the seam (see Photo 6). Allow just enough solder to flow into the joint to hold it together.

After soldering all these spots, your structure should be rigid enough to hold its shape. Gently remove the masking tape. Now you can continue soldering the rest of the seams, working your way around the structure in a step-wise motion, a half-inch or so at a time. Hold the iron and solder in place just long enough to fill the seam and form a smooth, rounded bead. If you stay too long, the solder may drip through the other side. Placing a wet paper towel on the other side up into the seam may prevent leaking solder and will assist your clean up. When all your seams are finished, wash off the flux with grease-cutting dishwashing liquid.

If you are soldering with mirrors in place,

such as attaching an eyepiece, you'll want to avoid getting flux inside your mirror system. First, clean all your surfaces, flux and coat the copper foil with solder, and clean again. Then dry tack your solder to create a continuous seam to seal the mirror system. Flux can then be applied to the exterior of these seams so that you can go back over them with solder to achieve a more attractive, finished seam.

Be careful to work in a well-ventilated area, handle the iron with care and unplug it when finished.

Working with Wood

Constructing a body or a stand out of wood can be as simple or as complex as you like. Even though one of the projects in this book requires a table saw to cut a rabbet, a simple flush cut edge would also suffice for a butt joint. Using a standard hand saw and a sand paper block, you can build a square cylinder kaleidoscope body by butting the edges together with glue.

62

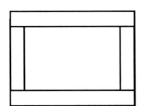

Butt

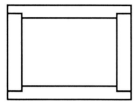

Rabbet

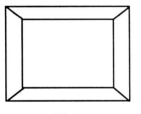

Miter

If you have a table saw, your cuts will be cleaner and more precise than with hand tools. Also, by adjusting the depth and angle of your cut, there are more options for joining the sides. You can also build cylinders that are triangular, hexagonal, tapered, or most any other shape. With more sophisticated tools and/or patience, the possibilities for ornamentation are also enhanced, such as carving, sculpting and inlay.

Your choice of woods is equally open. Thickness, stability, appearance and cost are all factors to be considered. Plywoods are available in many thicknesses and grades, some with attractive veneers. Pine is very accessible and can be stained many ways. Hardwoods are more expensive, but can be ordered from specialty lumber shops that can often plane it to your thickness specifications.

For best all around joining, use carpenter's wood glue. Clamps, weights, or even rubber bands can be used to achieve a tight seam. If you want to finish the wood with stain or clear finish, don't wipe the glue seams when wet. Rather, shave off excess glue with a knife and sand all over before finishing. There is a variety of stains, oils and finishes on the market, most of which will handsomely bring out the beauty of the grain and effectively protect it from years of handling.

It should go without saying that power-tools deserve respect. When working with small pieces of wood, keep your fingers away from moving blades by using push sticks or other aids. Bear in mind, too, that wood dust is good for neither your lungs nor your eyes. Wear an appropriate dust mask when working wood—and even consider wearing a respirator when sawing exotic species with powerful resins, such as walnut and cedar. Safety glasses should be a standard part of your attire.

Plastics and Metals

The plastic and metal projects in this book use standard, commercially available components. Generally, a diameter of tube or pipe is chosen that has commonly available fittings for the end pieces.

When cutting or drilling these materials, make sure you are using a blade or drill bit that is designed for that specific use. As always, power tools are more efficient and precise than hand tools, but both require caution and the usual safety practices.

There are many interesting materials worth exploring for your designs. Refer to the source guide in this book to get you started. Options for joining are varied, from gluing and welding to custom threading. Metals are usually polished and lacquered, but can be finished in many other ways, such as soldering, etching and enameling. Plastics can be altered for effect using coloration, texturing, and heat, among others. Experimenting with materials and techniques leads to new design possibilities.

Paper & Plastic Scope for Kids

Children have a natural appreciation for the "magic" of the kaleidoscope. There are many children who might apprentice themselves to a sorcerer just to learn how to craft this fascinating toy. Although this design uses only safe and simple materials for young hands, the skills and scientific principles acquired in the process are more than mere child's play. And the possibilities for design variation would challenge a wizard's imagination!

Materials List

Potato chip container - 9-3/4" tall, 3-1/8" diameter

2 plastic end caps (the 2nd from another chip container)

3" x 3" piece of 0.03" thick butyrate plastic

8" x 10" piece of 0.015" thick butyrate plastic

6" x 8-15/16" piece of white mat board

1/2" x 8-1/2" strip of corrugated cardboard

Packing material (styrofoam sheet or thick fabric)

Objects for viewing (plastic beads & fragments, trinkets, paper clips, etc.)

Spray adhesive

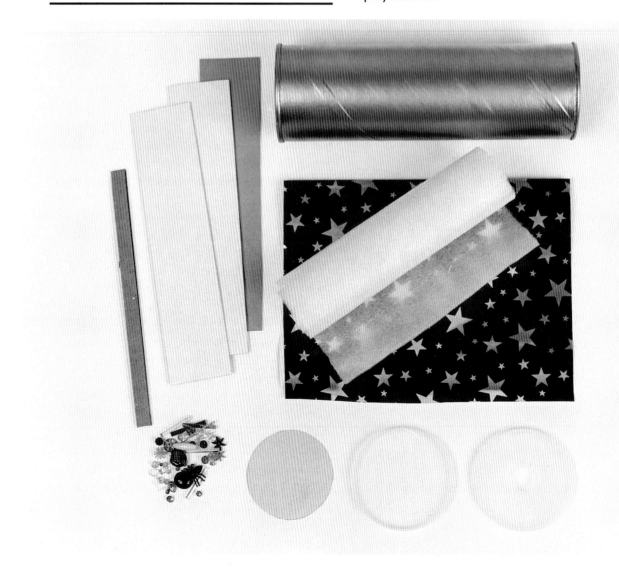

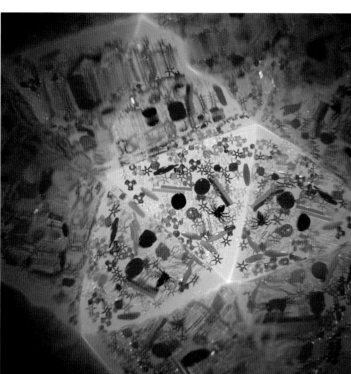

Here's how your scope might look on the inside.

Photo 1

1. To prepare the potato chip container, remove (and eat?) the chips. Cut out the bottom with a can opener. This end will be used for the eye piece cap. Wipe out the inside of the tube so that it is as clean as possible.

2. Decorate the tube. Use your imagination. You could spray paint it, cover it with paper and draw on it, wind ribbons or twine around it, cover it with cloth, or wrap it with gift wrapping paper (as shown in Photo 1).

3. Make the eyepiece using one of the plastic end caps. Cut a hole, traced from a dime, in the center with small scissors or a utility knife (as

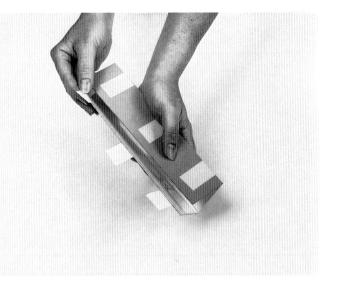

Photo 3

shown in Photo 2). Then cut a 2" x 2" piece of the thinner plastic (0.015" butyrate) and tape it to the inside of the cap to cover the hole. This will prevent any possible loose objects from the other end from falling in your eye. Now, snap it onto one end of the tube. (You may want to glue it in place.)

4. To create the mirrors, first spray the white side of the mat board with an even coat of adhesive—not too much. Then press the thin (0.015) plastic onto it. Mark three adjacent rectangles, lightly with a pencil, on the plastic, each measuring 2" x 8-15/16". Cut these three strips as

Photo 2

Photo 4

66

Photo 5

neatly as you can with scissors or a utility knife.

    5. To assemble the mirror system, lay the three mirrors, shiny side down, next to each other with 1/16" gaps between each long edge. Then tape across them with three 8" parallel strips of masking tape, so that you can fold the mirrors together and tape the last seam (as shown in Photo 3).

    6. Wrap the assembled mirror system with packing material until it fits snugly into the tube. (See Photo 4.) Push it in until it fits flush with the eye piece.

    7. To create the object chamber, cut a 2-

Photo 7

3/4" diameter circle from the 0.03" plastic with scissors. Then place it on top of the mirror system (as shown in Photo 5). Form the corrugated cardboard strip into a circle and place it on top of the plastic disc (as shown in Photo 6).

    8. Pour some objects into this chamber (see Photo 7), but leave about 1/3 of the space empty so they can move around. Then snap the other end cap over the end to seal the object chamber. This cap can be removed to change the objects, or even left open to view the world through a teleidoscope. But for the kaleidoscopic effect, rotate the tube and watch the patterns change as the objects tumble.

Variations

    Just like any other design in this book, all the major elements can be varied to create exciting new combinations and effects.

    There are many sorts of cardboard tubes available: wrapping paper tubes, carpet and industrial ream tubes, even cardboard salt containers. End pieces can be fabricated from cardboard, and have different sized and shaped eye holes. The mirror angles can be variously configured. And, of course, there are always new objects to consider for the chamber: string, wood chips, pasta, ball point pen springs, rubber bands, styrofoam balls…virtually any small object that has interesting color, shape, texture and lighting qualities.

Photo 6

WHIRLING BUBBLE SCOPE FOR ALL AGES

*T*his wacky scope appeals to the child in all of us. It is composed primarily of found objects, and is quick and easy to make. Children can assemble it safely by substituting the plastic/cardboard reflectors used in the first project. The amazing special effect created by the pinwheel whirling behind the foaming bubbles is well worth an hour's effort.

Interior view.

Materials List

Large plastic tumbler
Pinwheel
3 2nd surface mirrors: 1-3/4" x 4-3/8" (or to fit)
Plexiglass or 0.03" butyrate sheet: 3-1/2" x 6-1/2"
Bubble pipe
2 straws: straight and coiled
12" of 12 gauge copper wire (or heavy coathanger)

1. Drill an eye hole in the bottom of the tumbler about 1/2" in diameter. Cut a circle of plexiglass (with coping saw) or butyrate (with scissors) to fit inside the bottom of the tumbler (about 2-3/4" diameter), and glue it in place with plastic cement.

Photo
1

2. Find a recessed edge or any place near the lip of the tumbler, and cut another plastic circle to fit (about 3-1/2"). Measure the distance between these two plastic circles to determine the mirror length.

3. Cut 3 mirrors to this length and 1-3/4" wide, and assemble (see next project). Glue one end of mirrors, centered over eye hole, to the plastic circle in the bottom of the tumbler with silicone.

4. Place the larger plastic circle over the mirrors and glue the edge to the tumbler with plastic cement (see Photo 1).

5. Masking tape the bubble pipe to the tumbler, pointing in to center. Then tape the straight straw about 2" beside it.
Bend the wire into a "T":
Tape the top of the T
around the lip of the tumbler. Now secure all of this with duct tape (see Photo 2).

6. Cutting the ends to fit, insert the coiled straw into the bubble pipe, and tape the other end to the straight straw.

7. Bend tip of wire 90° and insert into stem of pinwheel, which has been cut to length so that the pinwheel will be visible through the mirrors. You can wrap the wire tip with duct tape to insure a snug fit.

8. The straight straw blows the pinwheel.

Drip bubble soap with a medicine dropper into the bubble pipe to blow bubbles into the viewing area.

Variations

The mirror configuration can be altered, even tapered. Pinwheels can be interchanged and embellished with different colors, sparklies, etc. Tape two together for a binocular effect. Look for other found objects.

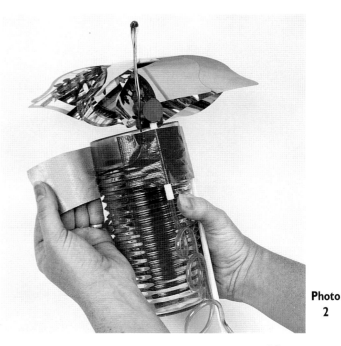

Photo
2

PLASTIC PIPE SCOPE FOR THE NOVICE

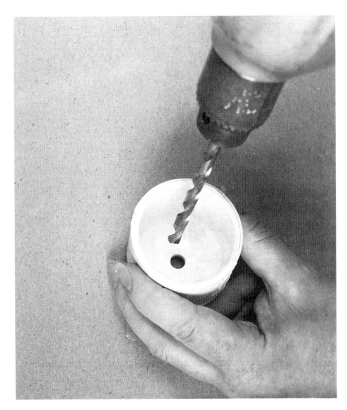

Photo 1

Photo 2

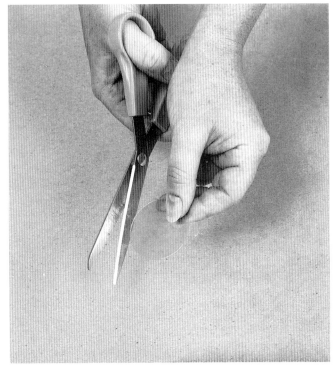

*F*rom computer micro chips to powdered orange drink, we've all seen how technologies developed for one use have found applications in many others. The scientists that invented PVC pipe may have imagined quite a few applications beyond plumbing, but kaleidoscopes? With ready-made fittings and tubing you can easily cut to any length, this design makes into a dandy scope that is durable, adaptable and professional-looking. And by substituting 1st surface mirrors with different angles and interchanging the objects in the open chamber, the quality and sophistication of your images is limited only by your imagination.

1. If you are cutting your own length of PVC pipe, you'll need to use a fine tooth blade, such as a hack saw or coping saw. Smooth the edges of the cut with a file and fine sand paper. Any ink lettering on the pipe can be rubbed off with steel wool.

2. In the center of the end cap, drill a 1/8" diameter hole to start the eye hole. Then change to a 5/16" bit and widen the hole (as shown in Photo 1).

Materials List

PVC pipe: 1-1/2" diameter, 9" long

PVC end cap: 1-1/2" diameter

PVC female adapter with threaded end:
1-1/2" diameter

1 sheet 0.03" Butyrate plastic: 2" x 4-1/2"

3 mirrors (2nd surface), each 1-1/8" x 10"

Styrofoam chips

3. From the sheet of butyrate, cut two circles, each 1-13/16" in diameter, and a third circle 1/2" in diameter (see Photo 2). Remove backing, if any.

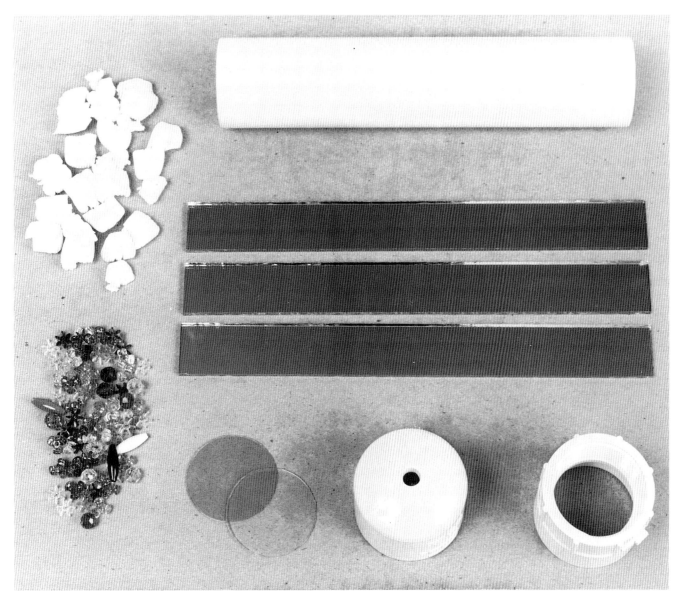

4. Using plastic cement, glue the small circle inside the end cap to shield the eye hole. Glue one of the larger circles inside the rim at the threaded end of the female adapter (as shown in Photo 3). Allow them to dry.

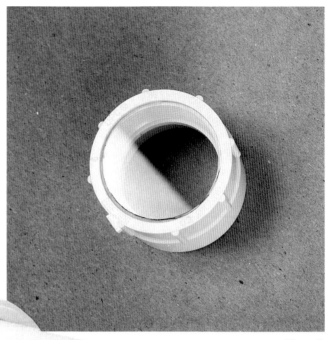

Photo 3

Interior view

Figure 1

Figure 2

5. Cut and clean the three mirror strips with window cleaner. Lay one of them on two strips of masking tape (see Figure 1). Position a second mirror (as shown in Figure 2), apply the tape and fold the mirror into a 60°. Position the third mirror so that the edges are aligned as in Figure 3, then wrap the tape all the way around. Further seal the assembly with duct tape, covering all the seams.

6. Place the end cap onto one end of the pipe, but not too tightly yet. Insert the mirror system partly into the pipe, and begin stuffing styrofoam chips equally around the three sides as you gradually insert the mirrors further. When the mirrors are fully inserted and packed, they should not slip out when inverted (see Photo 4). Mirrors should now be flush with the open end of the tube. Adjust the end cap (eye piece) to achieve this, if necessary.

Photo 4

Photo 5

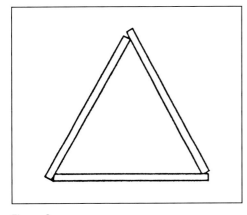

Figure 3

7. Place objects in the chamber (Photo 5) until they fill about 2/3 of the space up to the inner rim. Now place the remaining butyrate circle onto the inner rim (Photo 6), covering the objects.

8. The tube can now be inserted into the upper portion of the chamber, completing the scope. You may want to glue the eye piece permanently in place. The object chamber can be removed any time with a simple twisting motion, and opened to fill with new objects. It can also be removed to use your scope as a teleidoscope.

Variations

The eye hole can be larger. The pipe can be longer and/or larger diameter. It can be painted, carved, or accessorized with glue-on objects, wrapped with twine, etc. The mirror system can be varied many ways (see "Principles of Design"). The removable butyrate circle in the object chamber can be interchangeable with other sorts of tinted or textured pieces—even faceted discs or curved lenses. These can also be used without any objects in the chamber to alter the teleidoscopic effect.

Photo 6

Photo 7

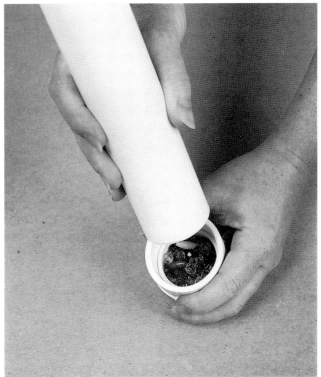

Classic Brass Teleidoscope

*Y*ou may notice the resemblance between this elegant scope and some of its antique predecessors. A major difference, however, is that this design has no object chamber. It is a teleidoscope. So whether you are viewing autumn foliage (below) or the beach at Waikiki (opposite), the world is your object chamber. Give this design a try, and you'll discover how such a simple approach can open so many exciting viewing possibilities.

Interior views through a 3-mirror system.

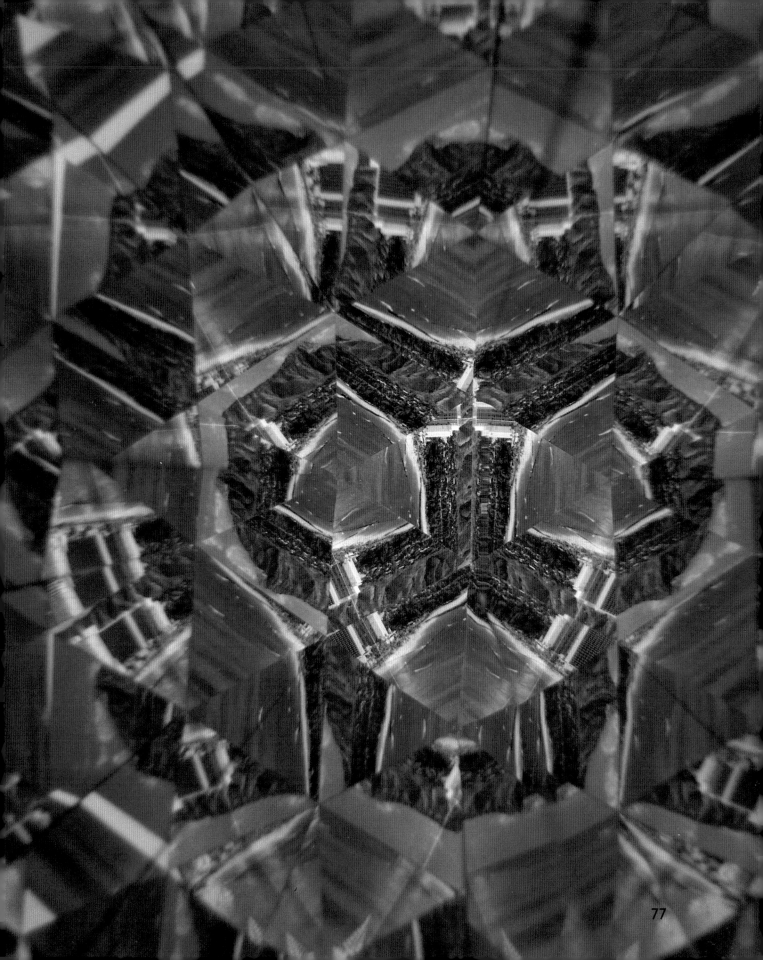

Materials List

Brass tube: 1-1/2" diameter, 8-1/4" long
3 1st surface mirrors: 1" x 8"
Plexiglass or glass sheet: approx. 2" x 4"
2 brass fittings
Packing material (styrofoam or thick cloth)

Note

If you have difficulty obtaining brass tube or fittings, consult the Source Guide in the back of this book. However, the measurements of all parts can be adjusted to suit whatever materials you can find.

1. If your brass tube has already been polished and lacquered, it is advisable to protect it during construction. Wrap it with newspaper, leaving 1/2" bare at each end, and secure with tape. If the brass is unfinished, you may also wrap it, take care in gluing, and buff and lacquer it after construction. Make sure all brass fittings are clean before gluing.

2. Cut the three mirrors, and assemble the mirror system as shown in the plastic pipe project.

3. Before you insert the mirror system into the tube, wrap it with packing material so that it will be centered and fit snugly. You can also stuff packing material, such as styrofoam strips or chips, around the mirrors as you insert them (as shown in Photo 1). One end of the mirrors should be almost flush with the tube, the other end recessed about 3/16".

Photo 2

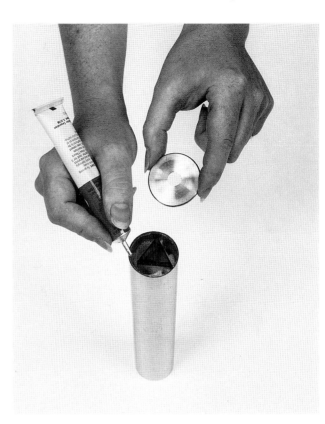

Photo 1

4. Cut two lenses, each 1-7/16" in diameter. Use a fine tooth coping saw to cut the plexiglass, or a glass cutter to cut glass, as described in "Construction Techniques." These should fit inside the brass tube. Clean the lenses.

5. Stand the tube up on the recessed end. Lay a lens on top of the mirrors so that it rests flush with the top of the tube. Using 5-minute epoxy and following the gluing directions on the container, glue the edge of the lens to the rim of the tube. (See Photo 2) Then glue the eye piece onto this end. Let dry.

6. Stand the tube up on the other end. If you want to conceal the packing material between the mirrors and the tube, you can stuff black paper over the top. Now lay the other lens on top of the recessed mirrors, and glue the edge to the inside of the tube to seal it (as shown in Photo 3). Avoid spilling glue onto the lens surface where it will be visible.

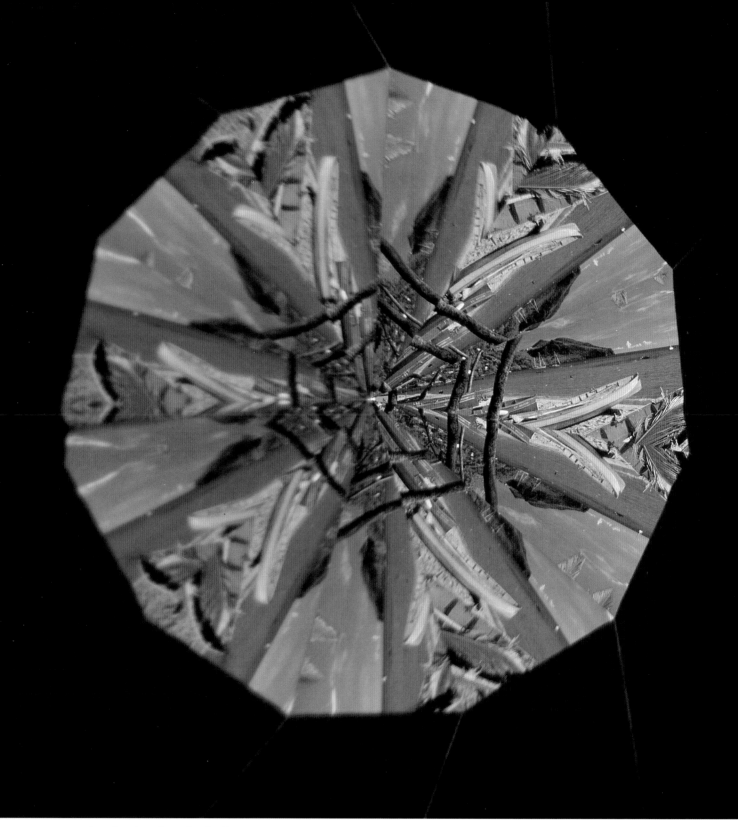

Interior view through a 2-mirror system.

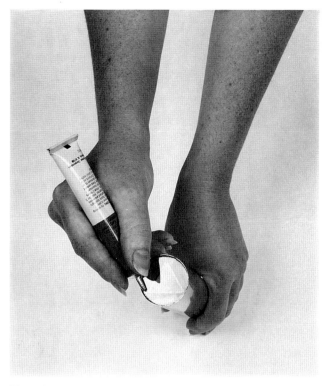

Photo 3

Photo 4

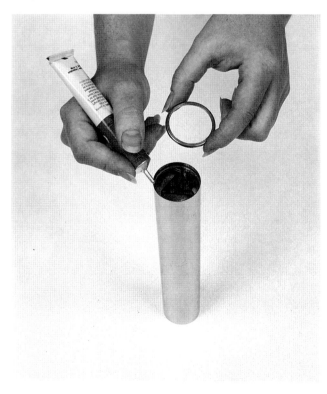

7. Glue the end cap onto this end (as shown in Photo 4). Let dry. Unwrap and/or finish the brass surfaces with polish and clear lacquer. Or try etching the brass decoratively.

8. You may want to cut out plastic discs of different tints and textures which can be slightly bent to fit into the recessed end of your scope. Leave a tab on one edge for easy removal. (See photo on page 76.)

Variations

Since the teleidoscope lacks the usual object chamber options, lenses become an important design element with which to experiment. In addition to colored, polarized and dichroic filters, various textures and facets on the surface of a lens can affect the image in many ways. Also, by attaching a curved lens—even a hemisphere—the potential for image distortion enters a new dimension.

If you were to thread the end of your tube for a screw-on end cap, you could make an assortment of interchangeable mirror systems. (see "Principles of Design.") The end lens would not be glued, but held in place by the end cap. Each mirror system would need to be measured carefully for a snug fit, without packing material. The photo (opposite) shows how a typical 2-mirror system might look.

Most of all, you can enjoy looking at usual sights in an unusual way. Moving objects are especially fascinating: water waves, smoke plumes, rustling leaves or flowers, billowing clouds, tongues of flame, flashing neon lights, etc. Imagine switching off between your opera glasses and a teleidoscope at the ballet, or viewing a fireworks display, or one of those Christmas baubles with the shake-up snow scene inside, or...

MINIATURE KALEIDOSCOPE PENDANT

The interior image has surprising detail (opposite right).

Actual scope length: 2-3/4"

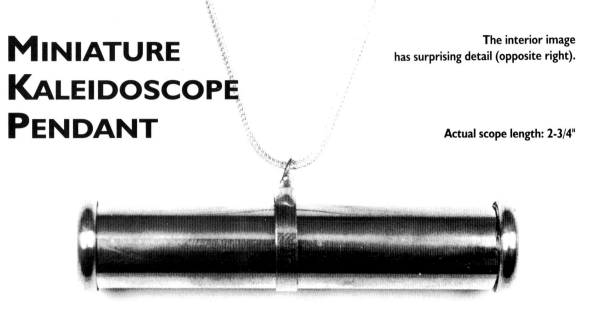

*T*he beauty of this tiny brass scope is its portability, but the quality of its image will amaze you. The more you grow to appreciate the joy of scope viewing, the more you'll wish you had one with you at various moments of the day. Whether you carry it on a necklace, a key chain, or fix it on a tie clip, the images are always within reach to soothe or stimulate. And as a teleidoscope, you can explore the many sights you encounter wherever you travel.

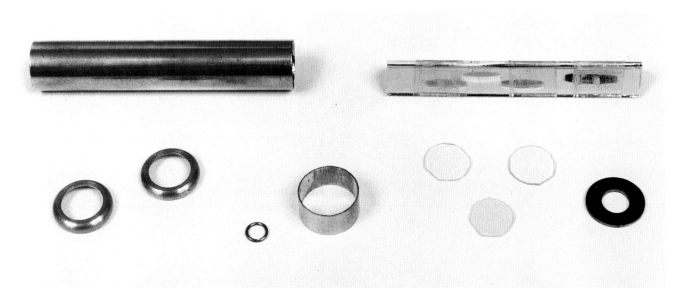

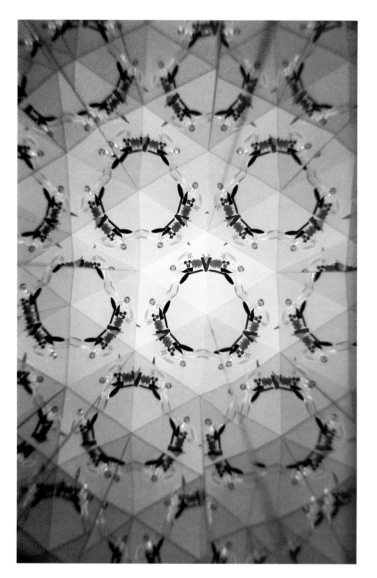

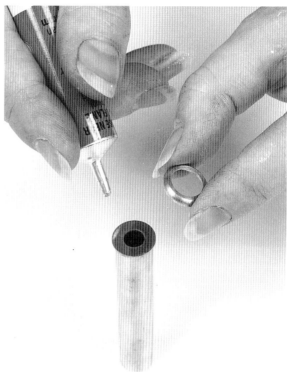

Photo 1

Photo 2

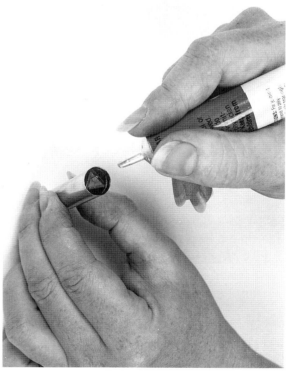

Materials List

Brass tube: 1/2" diameter, 2-3/4" long
3 1st surface mirrors: 3/8" x 2-3/8"
2 brass fittings: 1/2" (lamp base rings)
Small brass eyelet ring
Brass collar: 9/16" diameter, 1/2" long
Brass washer: 1/2"
0.03" butyrate or thick acetate sheet: 1" x 1"
Plano-convex lens: 10 mm x 90 mm FL

1. Follow the procedures concerning brass surfaces as described in the brass teleidoscope project.

2. Cut and assemble the three mirrors. You can align the seams more easily with household cellophane tape. Then wrap the mirror assembly with duct tape until it fits snugly inside the brass tube.

3. You can use the optical lens from a peep hole "door viewer," or order one from a supplier in the Source Guide. If it is plastic and larger than 15/32" diameter, you can file it down to size.

4. Apply a thin bead of 5-minute epoxy around the outer perimeter on the flat side of the lens. Then glue it, centered, on the washer. Let dry.

5. Apply a bead of epoxy on one of the rims of the brass tube. Carefully insert the lens and washer, curved surface facing inside, to glue it in place. Apply a bead of epoxy inside the lip of a brass fitting, and glue it over top (see Photo 1). Let dry.

6. Insert mirrors into tube. With scissors, cut two circles from the 1" square plastic sheet, each 15/32" in diameter. Place one of these on top of the mirrors inside the tube, and glue it in place (as shown in Photo 2). Avoid getting glue on the mirrors or in the viewing area of the plastic circle. Let dry.

7. The brass collar can be cut from tubing. Solder the small eyelet onto the collar (see Photo 3), although not in position around the tube as shown. After cleaning the ring and collar assembly, it should be placed around the tube (as shown).

8. Place small beads and fragments of broken stained glass into the object chamber (as shown in Photo 4). Fill about halfway full.

Photo 3

Photo 4

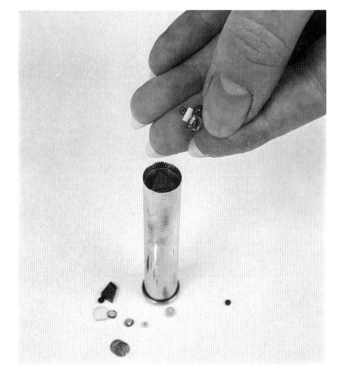

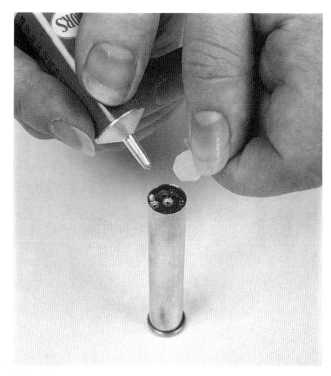

Photo 5

Photo 6

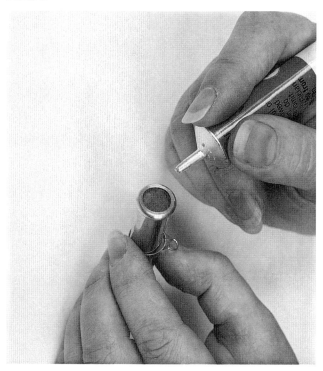

9. Frost the other plastic circle using fine sandpaper until it is uniformly cloudy and translucent.

10. Apply a bead of epoxy on the rim of the brass tube (see Photo 5), taking care not to glue any of the objects in the chamber. Gently place the frosted circle into the rim, so that it is perfectly flush with the top of the tube. Let dry.

11. Apply a bead of epoxy inside the lip of the other brass fitting, and glue it in place over the end of the object chamber (as shown in Photo 6). Let dry.

12. You may want to polish this brass scope every so often. A protective coat of clear lacquer is not advisable, since the collar around the tube will scratch it off unevenly, leaving marks to tarnish. Another option would be to solder the eyelet ring directly onto the tube.

Variations

To make a teleidoscope with this design, cut the mirrors 1/16" shorter than the brass tube. Use clear plastic lenses (not curved) on the ends, and follow the same basic procedures used in the brass teleidoscope project. There's no need to recess the object end for extra lenses, although permanently attaching a curved or hemispheric lens to the object end would produce interesting effects.

You also have the option of employing different sorts of mirror systems in either kaleidoscope or teleidoscope. The scope is probably too small to incorporate the option of interchangeable mirror systems, although you could carry several of these scopes with you—each with its own system. If a sheet of brass or copper were formed into a cone, a tapered mirror system could be accommodated.

WONDERFUL WOODEN SCOPE

*A*s simple as making a box, this woodworking project shows you the basics so you can go on to all sorts of more ambitious design variations. You'll also be introduced to a unique mirror system: two tapered mirrors that produce a "chorus line" effect. Wood has such warmth and natural beauty, we were inspired to fill our object chamber with a mixture of earthy baubles amongst the glittery ones: stones, sea shells, mother-of-pearl, bamboo and crystals.

Materials List

2 pieces of wood: 1/4" x 1-3/4" x 9"

2 pieces of wood: 1/4" x 1-1/2" x 9"

2 pieces of wood: 1/4" x 5/16" x 1-1/4"

1 piece of wood: 1/4" x 1-3/4" x 1-3/4"

2 1st surface mirrors: 1-1/4" x 7-7/8"

1 piece of 1/16" window glass: 1" x 1"

1 piece of 1/16" window glass: 1-1/4" x 1-1/4"

1 piece of white plexiglass: 1-1/4" x 1-1/4"

2 pieces of white plexiglass: 1/2" x 1-1/4"

5" of 14 gauge brass wire

5" of double face glazing tape

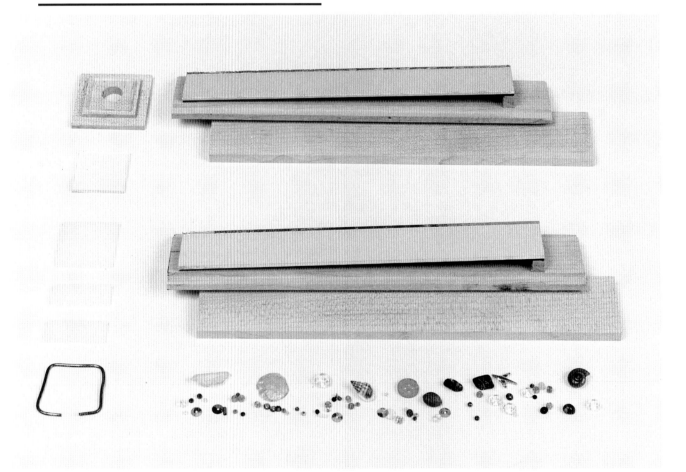

1. On a table saw, cut two pieces of 1/4" stock (most any wood you like) to 1-3/4" x 9". Set your saw to a 1/8" depth of cut, and rip cut a 1/4" rabbet down each long side. (See "Basic Construction Techniques" for other joinery options.) Now cut two more pieces of 1/4" stock

Photo 1

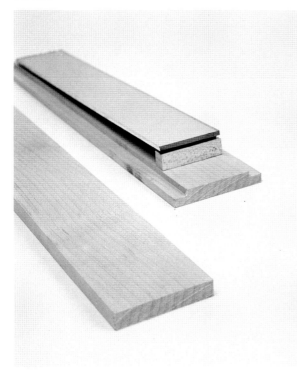

to 1-1/2" x 9". (Photo 1) You may want to paint one side of each of these two plain panels flat black for a more striking effect. Note all edges to be glued and mask these margins from the paint for a better glue joint. Lightly sand new edges.

2. Carefully, using a push stick, rip cut a length of 1/4" stock to a width of 5/16". Then cut two lengths, 1-1/4" each. These are the mirror blocks.

3. Mark one end of each of the two rabbet-cut pieces with two parallel lines: 7/8" and 1-1/4" in from the end. Glue the 1/4" surface of each mirror block inside these lines.

4. Cut two mirrors, 1-1/4" x 7-7/8" each. Install the mirrors carefully, with one end flush with the mirror block (as shown in Photo 2) using 1-1/4" strips of double face glazing tape.

5. Run a bead of glue into all four rabbet cuts, and distribute evenly with your finger. Set the two mirror panels on top of a plain panel (see Photo 3), then gently lay the other plain panel into the rabbet cuts on top. Secure the assembly with rubber bands (see Photo 4) and allow 4 hours to dry. If you plan to use a natural wood finish, don't wipe the excess glue at the seams. Instead, shave off excess with a knife after it has dried, then sand.

6. To cut the eye piece, cut a 1-3/4" x 1-

Photo 2

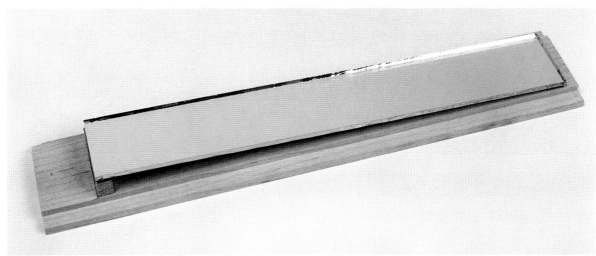

3/4" piece of 1/4" stock, then cut a 1/4" rabbet, 1/8" deep, all the way around. Drill a 1/2" hole in the center (see Photo 5), then sand all new edges.

7. Cut a 1" square of window glass, clean it, and glue it over the inside of the eye hole (see Photo 6) with silicone. After this has dried, you can glue this eye piece into the end of the tube without the mirror blocks using wood glue (see Photo 7). Allow it to dry, then sand the whole body to your liking.

8. Cut a 1-1/4" square of window glass, clean it, and glue it against the mirror blocks (see Photo 8) with silicone. This forms the inside object chamber window.

9. Cut two pieces of 1/2" x 1-1/4" white plexiglass spacers using a fine tooth coping saw or hack saw. Glue these in place above the mir-

Photo 3

Photo 4

ror blocks (see Photo 9) with silicone.

10. Cut a 1-1/4" square of white plexiglass for the object chamber lid. This is dropped into place, but never glued (see Photo 10).

11. Bend a piece of 14 gauge brass wire around a 1-1/16" square block to make the lock spring (see Photo 11). Then force it into place

Photo 7

Photo 5

Photo 6

"Chorus line" effect inside the tapered two-mirror system (opposite).

Interior view of standard three-mirror system (below).

Photo 8

Photo 10

Photo 9

Photo 11

over the lid (as shown in Photo 12).

12. To insert and change objects, simply unspring the lid and replace it. The chamber may, of course, be left open for use as a teleidoscope. This would also include viewing 35 mm slides or film strips.

Variations

You may want to incorporate different woods in the body—perhaps add some carving or inlay, or try different stains. The corners can be rounded with a router as a more comfortable handheld feature. Obviously, wood allows you much freedom to experiment with different sizes and shapes.

Mirror systems can be varied any number of ways. For a standard three-mirror system, join three strips of mirror, 1-1/6" x 7-7/8" each. Attach a corrugated cardboard shim with two long strips of double face glazing tape (see Photo 13). When assembling the body, leave out the mirror blocks. Slide the mirrors into the body, and install both end piece assemblies as before. For tighter angled mirror systems, you may need to adjust the size and position of the eyehole.

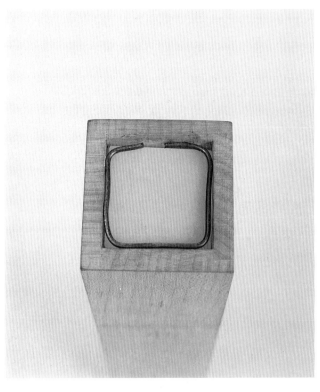

Photo 12

Photo 13

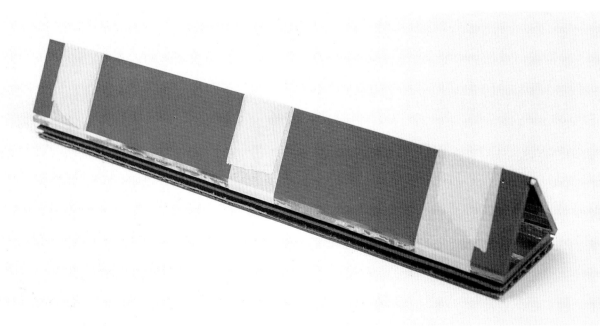

STAINED GLASS TWO-MIRROR SCOPE

There is much beauty in the simplicity of this scope—inside and out. Except for the foil and solder, it is composed entirely of glass. The colors you choose for your scope can be attuned to the disposition and yearnings of your spirit, or to the friend for whom you make it. And the two-mirror system, preferred by many, produces the spectacular "mandala" image that is sure to hold you spellbound.

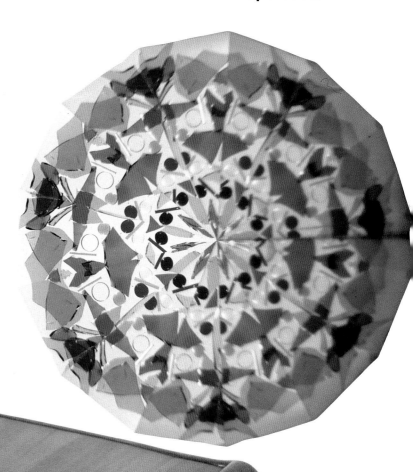

Three interior views of two-mirror "mandala" images.

Materials List

4 strips of stained glass: 1-1/4" x 8"

2 1st surface mirrors: 1-3/16" x 7-1/2"

1 mirror glass: 5/8" x 7-1/2"

1 piece of stained glass: approx. 1-1/2" square

1 piece of clear glass: approx. 1-1/2" square

1 piece of clear glass: approx. 1-1/4" square

1 small scrap of clear glass for eye piece

1 strip of black velvet or felt: 5/8" x 7-1/2"

1. Cut four strips of stained glass, 1-1/4" x 8" each. (See "Basic Construction Techniques" for all stained glass assembly.) Clean the glass, and wrap all the edges with copper foil (see Photo 1). Brush on the paste flux, then coat all the foil with solder. Clean off the flux.

2. Assemble the four panels into a cylinder and secure them with masking tape. Tack solder the four corners on each end (as shown in Photo 2). The structure should hold its shape as you gently remove the masking tape. Now you can flux and solder all the seams. Clean off flux, inside and out, when you're done.

3. Cut two mirrors, 1-13/16" x 7-1/2" each. Cut another strip of mirror or glass 5/8" x 7-1/2". Cover this smaller strip with an equal strip of

Photo 1

black velvet or felt using spray adhesive (see Photo 3).

   4. Lay the two larger mirrors, 1st surface side down, 1/8" apart. Gently apply duct tape down the seam (as shown in Photo 4). Cut a 7-1/2" length of duct tape about 2" wide, and lay it

Photo 2

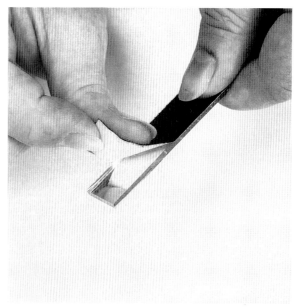

Photo 3

on a table, sticky side up. Lay the smaller panel, black surface up, in the center of the tape. Fold the larger mirrors into an acute angle, tape facing outside, and place them over the black panel to create tight seams with the black panel fitting flush inside the top of the "V." Wrap the tape

Photo 4

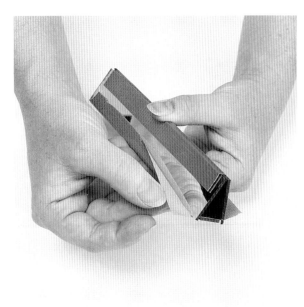

Photo 5

Photo 7

around both seams (as shown in Photo 5). The mirror assembly should fit snugly inside the square cylinder. Wrap more tape if necessary. The mirrors should be flush with one end of the cylinder, recessed on the other. (See Photo 6)

    5. Cut a piece of clear glass that will just fit

inside the recessed end of the cylinder, approximately 1-1/4" square. Mark the actual opening to allow for any inconsistencies, and leave space for the foil. Clean the glass square, wrap it with foil, coat the foil with solder, clean it again, and then tack solder it into the recessed end of the cylin-

Photo 6

Photo 8

der at all four corners (as shown in Photo 7).

6. Cut a piece of stained glass to fit the flush end of the cylinder. Then cut it diagonally into two pieces. Cut an arc inside the long edge of each piece, refining the edge by chipping at it with the teeth of your cutter (see Photo 8). Now cut a small football-shaped piece of clear glass that will fit inside these two arcs. Foil and join these three pieces into a square to serve as the eye piece.

7. Clean the eye piece, then dry tack it onto the flush end of the cylinder. Flux is not used until the end is sealed, so as not to foul the mirrors, but can be used afterwards to make a prettier seam (see Photo 9).

8. Cut a piece of clear glass to fit the recessed end of the cylinder. Prepare it for joining. Fill the object chamber about 1/2 to 2/3 full with small colored glass fragments and globules, or anything else you like. The object chamber will remain closed, so choose carefully. Dry tack the clear square over the end using the same method as the eye piece. After cleaning away the exterior flux, the solder can be finished with copper sulphate if you wish.

Variations

This basic design lends itself to many variations: size and shape of the eye piece; size, shape and color of the body; most any sort of mirror configuration; perhaps a hinged lid covering the object chamber so that the objects may be changed; an object chamber that has side-lighting with an opaque end and clear sides; using filtered glass in the object chamber or in place of the black mirror panel; objects that tumble inside the entire length of the mirror system...explore the possibilities!

Photo 9

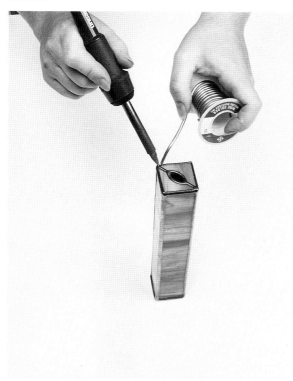

Photo 10

STAINED GLASS WITH WHEELS

Stained glass lends itself beautifully to scope making. This design exploits the properties of color and light with glass wheels that function as external object chambers. Basic stained glass technique enables easy construction of the wheels in both two and three dimensions, and all are interchangeable. Select the colors of glass you like, practice your joinery skills, and give this scope a whirl.

Materials List

Body
3 panels of stained glass: 1-1/2" x 8"
2 clear glass triangles: 1-7/16" sides
3 1st surface mirrors: 1-1/4" x 7-7/8"
Brass rod: 1/8" diameter, 3" long
3/8" brass ball with threaded hole
2 brass eyelets (for legs)

Chamber
6 stained glass rectangles: 1/2" x 1-1/2"
2 clear glass hexagrams: 1-1/2" sides
Brass tube: 1/8" diameter, 3/4" long

Disc
Several stained glass pieces to fill 3" circle
Brass eyelet

Photo 1

The Body

1. Foil and join the stained glass panels into a triangular cylinder. (See "Construction Techniques.")

2. Thread one end of the brass rod to accommodate the brass ball. Solder the other end of the rod into one of the seams at the end of the stained glass cylinder. Leave 1-3/8" of the rod extending beyond the end of the cylinder.

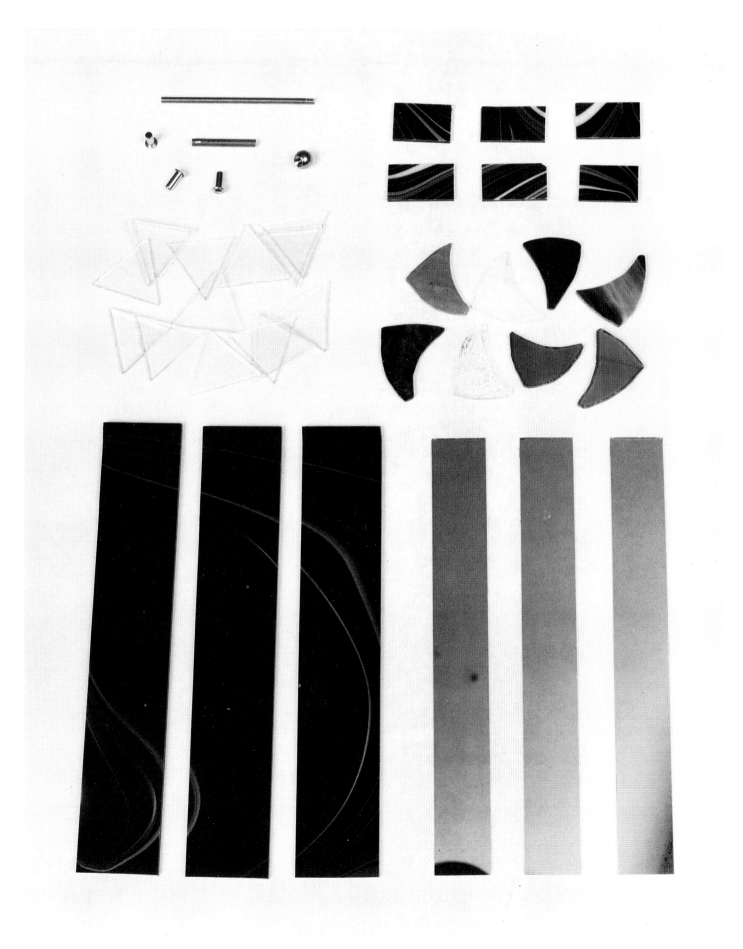

Interior view of flower disc
through 3-mirror system (above).

Chamber wheel with stained glass contents
and two detachable discs..

3. Now solder the two brass eyelets into the other two seams of the cylinder at the same end (see Photo 1). Flux and smooth out all solder seams, and clean.

4. Cut and assemble the mirrors.

5. Insert the mirror system into the cylinder, using packing material to center it with a snug fit (see Photo 2). Leave equal margins of recess at each end of the cylinder.

6. Foil both clear glass triangles, and solder them into each end of the cylinder to seal the mirror system (see Photo 3). Be careful to use dry solder techniques, so as not to foul the mirrors. Foil can be added to secure the seal. Refine the seams, and clean. This completes the body.

The Chamber

1. Foil and join the six stained glass rectangles into a hexagram (see Photo 4) by spot soldering the corners.

2. After you've cut the two clear glass hexagrams, frost one of them with fine sand paper to make it translucent.

3. Cut both of the hexagrams into sixths, creating six triangles from each (see Photo 5). Carefully chip or grind off one corner of each triangle to accommodate a 3/16" hole for the

Photo 2

Photo 3

brass tube in the center.

4. Foil all 12 triangles, and join back into two hexagrams, one clear and one frosted, each with center hole space.

5. Solder one of the hexagrams to the stained glass side assembly. Insert the brass tube upright into the hole, and solder in place. Solder the seams between the six stained glass sides. Clean the interior. (Note: Two eyelets could be used in place of the tube.)

6. Fill the chamber about half full with objects: stained glass fragments, beads, etc.

7. Dry solder the other hexagram to complete the chamber (see Photo 6). Then finish all seams, including the brass tube at the center.

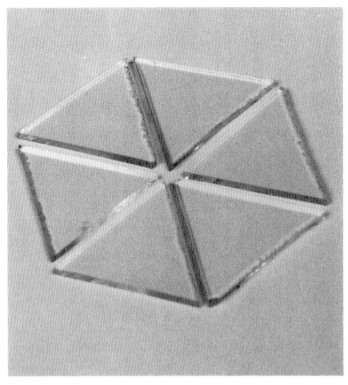

Photo 5

Photo 4

Photo 6

Examples of discs using stained glass techniques and sandwiched panes.

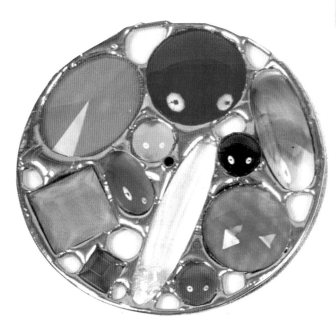

Discs

Discs can be constructed in many ways. For a stained glass disc, draw a 3" circle and divide it into segments. Choose your colors and textures. Cut the pieces using your pattern, leaving a 3/16" hole in the center to accommodate the brass eyelet (see Photo 7). Foil and join.

Discs can also be joined in this manner using faceted glass and plastic, agates and crystals. Explore other materials to incorporate.

You can sandwich objects (flowers, feathers, butterfly wings, etc.) between two panes of plexiglass. Tape the rims and drill a hole in the center.

Another technique involves casting objects in plastic resin in the form of a disc, which can be drilled with a hole in the center. Add the catalyst to some "casting resin," pour a layer into a round mold, lay your objects on top, pour the second layer, and let cure (see "Source Guide," and follow product directions).

Photo 7

Variations

The mirror configurations—hence body shape—can ve varied. Materials for the body can also vary, although using stained glass for the wheels is rather ideal. The body and the wheels can be ornamented with sculpted beads of solder.

The turning chamber can be mounted on an axis turned 90° so that objects are seen from the side, which would need to be clear. A three-dimensional wheel can also incorporate stained glass, crystals, globules, etc. on its surface rather than inside a chamber.

Turning object chambers can be interchangeable, each with different contents, or have a hinged door to empty and refill contents.

By constructing a hollow disc with plexiglass and epoxy, fluids of different densities and colors (mineral oils, glycerines, etc.) can be contained and viewed as they slowly swirl.

TAPERED SCOPE WITH SPHERES

Here's a contemporary variation on the parlor scope, featuring a unique mirror system that produces a three-dimensional, spherical image. This particular design uses marbles as viewing objects, to heighten the effect, but even a road map would look like a globe through these mirrors. And the eye piece at the top is so large you can see prismatic reflections of your eyes peering at the sphere from all angles.

Materials List

3 Stained glass panels: 1-3/4" x 4-3/4" x 8"

3 1st Surface mirrors: 1-1/8" x 3-7/8" x 7-3/4"

Clear glass triangle: 4-3/4" each side

Split ring (key ring): 1" diameter

Large playing marble ("bunker"): approx. 1"

1/8" Brass rod: 12" long

3 3/8" Brass balls with threaded holes (optional)

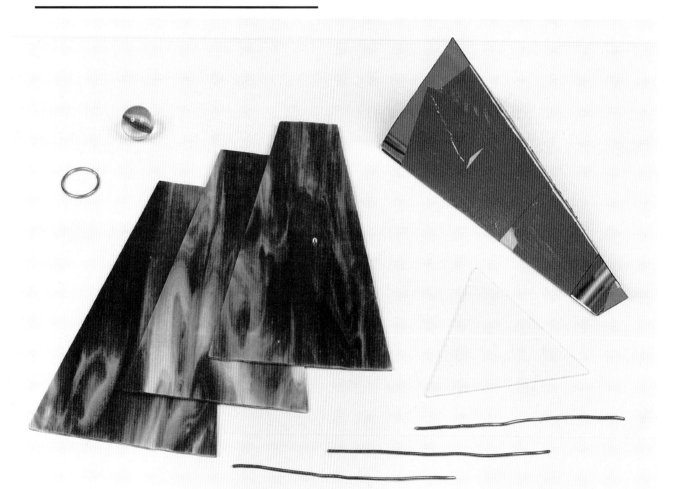

1. Cut the three stained glass panels. Clean and copper foil the edges. Solder them together (see "Construction Techniques") into a pyramid.

2. Cut the brass rod into thirds. Bend each one into a relaxed "V", to serve as legs. If you can't find the brass balls to screw into the legs as feet, hammer the ends into a tight curve.

3. Solder the three legs into the lower seams of the stained glass pyramid (as shown in Photo 1). Bend the legs as necessary to adjust the pyramid toward a balanced upright position.

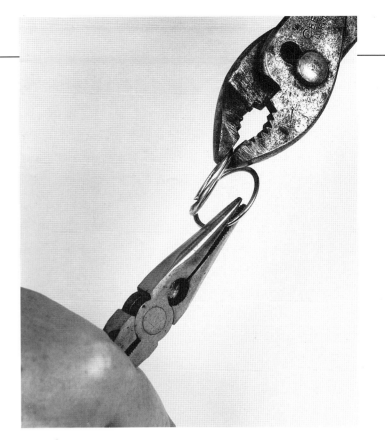

Photo 2

Photo 3

Photo 1

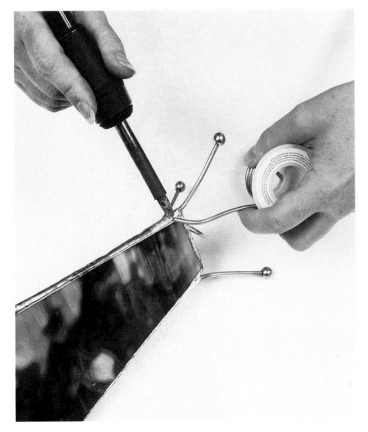

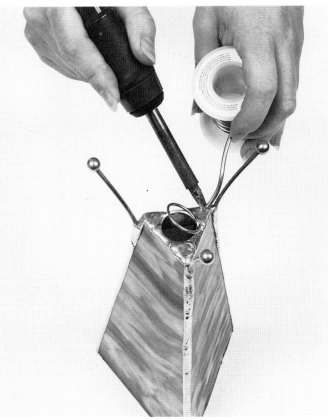

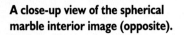

A close-up view of the spherical marble interior image (opposite).

Tapered scope with a variety of spheres which can be placed in or under the object chamber.

4. Pry open the split ring to about 40° to accommodate the marble with spring tension (see Photo 2).

5. Solder the split ring onto the legged end of the pyramid (see Photo 3). Clean off the flux, then fill in the gaps at the corners of the triangle with copper foil. Cover with solder, and clean off the flux again.

6. Cut and assemble the mirrors into a corresponding pyramid with duct tape. Add packing material (such as styrofoam sheets or felt) to the sides until the mirror assembly rests comfortably centered inside the stained glass pyramid (see Photo 4). Install the mirrors so that they fit snugly inside the body.

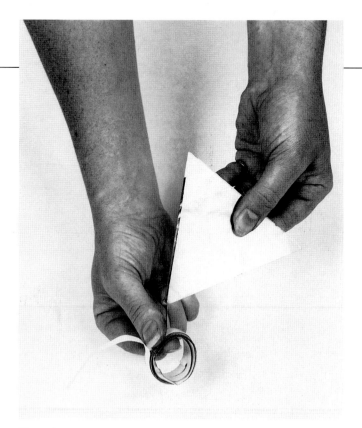

Photo 5

Photo 4

Photo 6

7. Foil the clear glass triangle (as shown in Photo 5). Coat with solder, clean, and dry solder the triangle onto the wide end of the stained glass pyramid, being careful to keep the mirrors clean as they are sealed.

8. Add copper foil to conform to the mirror opening. Flux and solder this margin around the viewing lens (as shown in Photo 6). Clean off flux.

9. Insert a marble into the split ring (see Photo 7). You can rotate the marble while viewing. You can also remove the marble, and place the scope over any image to view it, whether it is table-top or handheld.

Variations

If you are not inclined toward stained glass fabrication, you can still execute this design with other materials. Any kind of wood in 1/8" thickness would substitute nicely. Plastics and metals would also lend themselves appropriately.

The object end of the scope could be left unobstructed by a split ring and marble. This would allow for better viewing of other objects.

A major option of interest is the mirror system. This need not be a 3-mirror arrangement. A tapered 4-mirror system also produces a spherical image, but with different facets.

While maintaining similar proportions, the overall dimensions of this design can be altered up and down. Even teleidoscopic dimensions can be explored more fully.

A scope of this kind could be fitted with any number of object chambers: turning on different axes, interchangeable, fluid-filled, etc.

Photo 7

Interior view of turn-tray through a 3-mirror system.

PARLOR SCOPE WITH TURN-TRAY

This unusual looking configuration could be fashioned in a number of stylistic presentations to suit any taste, and the dynamics of the design are worthy of diversification. The table-top format, with a "lazy susan" large enough to display an array of personal talismans and memorabilia, can be a potent vehicle for self-knowledge and meditation. Revolve the tray, reflect on the images, resolve and evolve your vision.

Materials List

Wooden base: 3/4" x 6" x 12"

Wooden dowel: 3" long, 1" diameter

CPVC pipe: 5" long, 1-1/8" diameter

PVC pipe: 10" long, 2" diameter

Plastic "lazy susan" turn-tray

3 1st surface mirrors: 1-3/8" x 9-3/4"

Clear plexiglass sheet: 2" x 4"

Packing material (styrofoam or cloth)

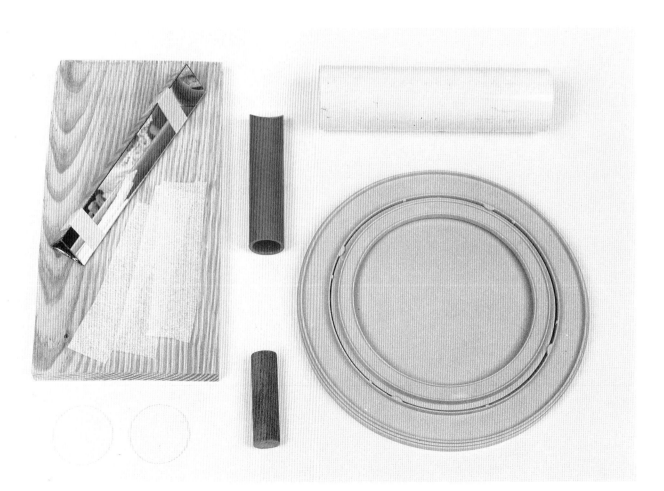

1. Shape one end of the CPVC pipe with a coping saw (see Photo 1) so that it will cradle the larger PVC pipe at an angle. Finish the edges of the cut with a rounded file for a nice tight fit.

2. Cut and assemble the mirrors.

3. Wrap the mirror system with sheets of styrofoam or thick cloth until it fits snugly, centered, inside the PVC pipe. Leave equal margins of recess at each end.

4. With a coping saw, cut 2 circles from the clear plexiglass sheet, each about 2" in diameter, to fit the inner diameter of the PVC pipe. The edges can be finished with a file.

5. With mirrors in place, glue each of the plexiglass circles into the recess of each end of the PVC pipe using plastic cement or 5-minute epoxy (see Photo 2). Let dry.

6. Using epoxy ribbon or glue, assemble the two plastic pipes together (as shown in Photo 3). Let dry.

7. Drill a small hole through one end of the rectangular base, and another into one end of the

Photo 2

Photo 1

Photo 3

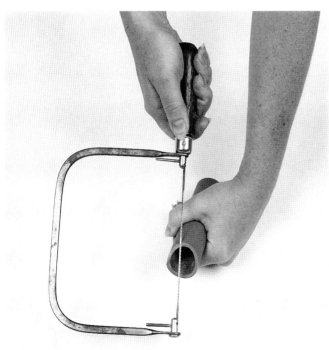

Photo 4

Photo 6

wooden dowel. Apply epoxy to that end of the dowel, insert a flat-headed wood screw up through the bottom of the base and screw it into the dowel, counter-sinking the head. Epoxy the CPVC pipe over the dowel and onto the base so that the scope barrel is angled slightly away from center. Let dry.

8. Trace a dime-size circle onto masking tape, cut it out, and stick it onto the center of the plexiglass eye piece at the upper end of the pipe. Mask off the entire lens on the other end, and

Photo 5

trim the circle neatly. The entire base is now ready to paint. This base was sprayed with faux granite paint, though you may choose another (see Photo 4). The eye hole will appear (as shown in Photo 5).

9. You may want to paint the turn-tray, or perhaps glue on some decorative paper as shown in our model. It should then be glued onto the base in position (as shown in Photo 6) with epoxy. Half of the tray should be in view through the scope.

Variations

The over-all design and materials can be varied greatly. The scope could be mounted on an arc that spans the tray, positioned overhead or moveable. Stained glass elements could be incorporated into finished hardwoods. Dimension and style are variables. The turn-tray could be motorized, perhaps with musical accompaniment.

Obviously, the mirror system can be configured many ways. A poly-angular system would be quite appropriate for this design. It would also be interesting to mount two scopes in binocular fashion, one focused on the advancing half of the tray—the other on the retreating half.

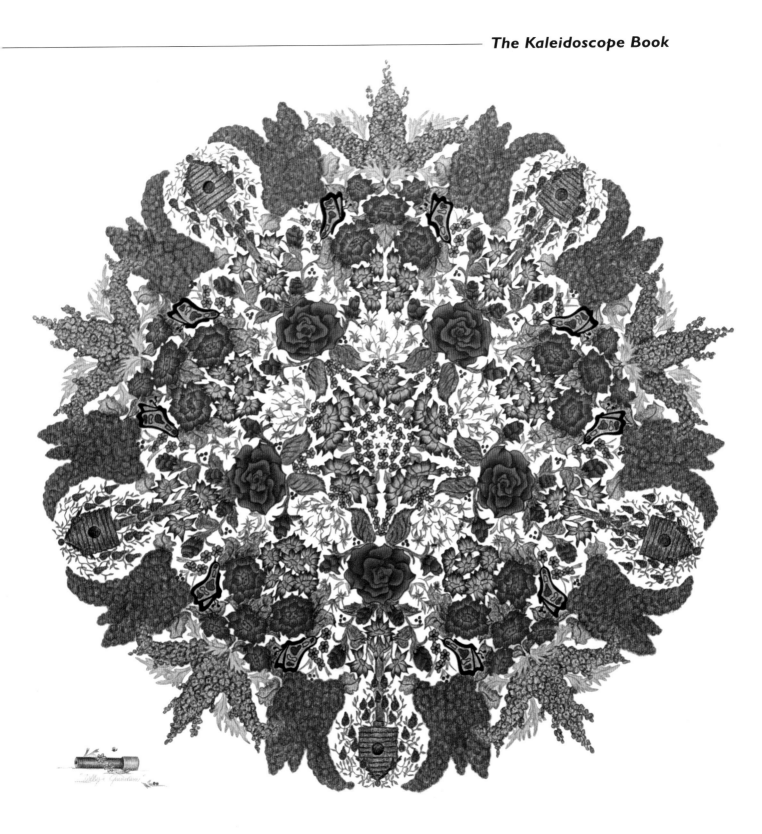

"Tilley's Garden," kaleidoscopic drawing by Betty Tribe

GIANT BACKYARD DOUBLE SCOPE

Just when you thought you might have mastered all the basic techniques, here's a bonus design gigantic enough to challenge any notions of what a scope might be. While primarily for children (constructed with adult supervision), the design implications are quite interesting. Think big!

Materials List

2 cardboard boxes used to house refrigerators (approx. 36" x 36" x 72")

Several rolls of heavy duty aluminum foil

Spray adhesive

Duct tape

Black paint

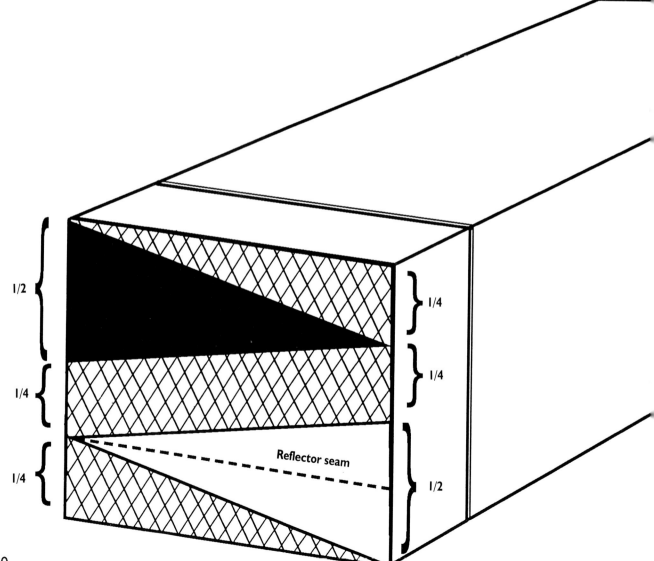

1/2

1/4

1/4

1/4

1/4

1/2

Reflector seam

1. Find the two large boxes. (Kids are usually quite good at this.)

2. Paint two opposing walls of one of the boxes black. Mark the ends into equal quarters (see diagram).

3. From the second box, cut four panels, approximately 36" x 72" each, or larger.

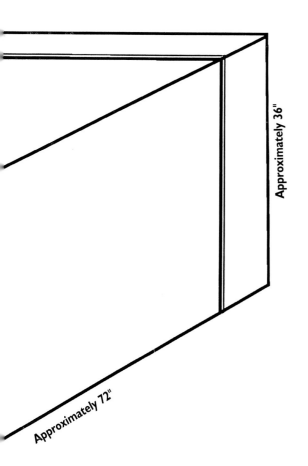

Approximately 36"

Approximately 72"

4. Spray one side of each of these four panels with spray adhesive, and carefully cover with sheets of aluminum foil (shiny side up) to create a smooth reflective surface. Wrap the foil around all the edges.

5. Duct tape two pairs of panels along their long edges, reflectors inward.

6. Insert these, one at a time, into the box so that the top of each "V" faces one of the black sides (see diagram). Observing the 1/4 and 1/2-way marks, secure them in place with duct tape. Add a filler strip at the base of each "V" to connect with the sides.

7. Trim any of the top and bottom panels of the box away from the reflective planes. Reinforce with duct tape.

8. Decorate your box however you wish. Keep it out of the rain if you want it to last.

9. Either end is the eye piece. Several children can play at these ends, looking at each other's faces, and waving objects at the viewing areas. Colorful windblown streamers, large graphics, flashlights, objects attached to a spinning bicycle wheel, and pet animals are but a few of the objects that can be viewed.

Variations

As always, mirror angles can be altered. Various systems can be housed in this cylinder—and more than two.

Size is not a limitation, especially if materials and reinforcement are upgraded. Lenses might be added to shield and magnify the images.

Kaleidoscopes:
Scientific Bases and the Need for Precision

by Ethan Allen, Ph.D.

Kaleidoscopes' recent re-emergence as an art form should not obscure the fact that they are instruments based on scientific principles.

A comparison of kaleidoscopes to architecture seems apt. While architecture is an art form that encourages creative expression, it is firmly rooted in sound engineering principles. Ignoring these foundations invites structural (and consequently aesthetic) failure; use of appropriate materials and sound design are fundamental to the field. Similarly, while kaleidoscopes permit a vast range of creativity and allow a significant role for personal taste, ignoring the optical and mathematical principles upon which the art is founded can only be detrimental to the kaleidoscopes. For kaleidoscope artists to angle reflectors whimsically, ignoring the issue of symmetry is as absurd as for architects to design whimsically, ignoring the issue of gravity.

While this need for precision in the creation of these marvelous devices is commonly understood by those who create kaleidoscopes (Dorothy Marshall suggests "kaleidoscopists"), it sometimes appears lacking in discussions of this art form. For example, I used to frequently hear the term "octascope" used to describe teleidoscopes with six-fold symmetry.

Derived from the Greek for eight, the term "octascope" can appropriately be applied to kaleidoscopes (of any type) showing eight-fold symmetry. The term "teleidoscope" (Greek, "distant form viewing") describes any scope through which things ("forms") at a distance are viewed; if one wishes to refer to eight-fold multiplicity of patterning in a teleidoscope, a term such as "octa-teleidoscope" would be descriptive. A little bit of basic research with a dictionary could have avoided the widespread use of an embarrassingly incorrect term.

Another common case of problematical terminology centers around what to call those things that one views through a kaleidoscopes. Various terms (e.g., pieces, viewing objects, colors, chips, bits) are routinely applied to several types of scopes, despite obvious inappropriateness. These terms were more widely applicable prior to the current renaissance that generated various types of scopes not containing the traditional bits of colored glass: teleidoscopes, scopes through which colored oils or LEDs are viewed, scopes making use of polarizing filters, etc. This proliferation created the need for a broadly applicable, yet accurate term.

While developing the Smithsonian traveling exhibit, Dorothy and I took this problem to her father, Dr. Robert Marshall, a classical language scholar, who pointed out that there exists a perfectly suitable term. Videnda (singular videndum), derived from the Latin for "that which should be viewed," can apply to the world at large (for teleidoscopes), solid pieces as well as liquids, unitary constructs (such as marbles or wheels) as well as multiple objects, achromatic as well as multi-hued things, LEDs in sound-actuated scopes, etc. Here again, a bit of simple research led to an appropriate solution.

The above examples have focused on terminology since creators, collectors, retailers, and others wishing to communicate about this

Beyond Creativity: Quality and Standards

by Dorothy Marshall

unique art form need to have a common vocabulary. But the needs for precision and accuracy extend into all phases of kaleidoscopes—design, construction, marketing, teaching—and these needs mandate that kaleidoscopists and other interested parties avail themselves of the resources around them to obtain the desired information. Libraries, colleges and universities, art associations, and artists themselves may be able to help you or to direct you to other sources that can do so. Don't settle for second-hand, hearsay information; if you have a question, research it until you are satisfied you have sufficient accurate and precise information.

The credibility of kaleidoscopic art is neither universal nor automatic. All too commonly kaleidoscopes are still regarded as kids' toys, without adequate appreciation of the subtlety and sophistication inherent in them. Too often those with little background in the area will teach classes, write articles, or even compose text for educational exhibits. Only through continually striving to educate themselves, their customers, and each other will kaleidoscopists and kaleidoscopes come to command the respect they deserve. And only through rigorous research and a commitment to precision and accuracy will real education occur.

Precision and accuracy in creating kaleidoscopes benefit the final work structurally, aesthetically, and optically. And solid research leading to precision and accuracy in descriptions of kaleidoscopic phenomena will enhance the credibility of the field and allow kaleidoscopists' potential contributions to art, mathematics, and science to be more fully realized.

Kaleidoscopists have particular obligations to those who will enjoy their work. Most importantly, they must provide a safe product. Unfortunately, safety is not always a given.

A good example is that most scopes need a protective eye piece. Its function is twofold: first, to keep dust and dirt from the reflector assembly; more importantly, however, is its role in protecting the user against possible eye injury should the scope be broken and have sharp, loose pieces inside. (People who drop a kaleidoscope don't always mention it, especially in a retail situation.) Obviously, plastic is the safe and appropriate material for this eye piece.

Nevertheless, I am aware of many instances where authors and artists are recommending and/ or using glass eye pieces. Such action invites disastrous repercussions—in addition to the horrifying specter of serious visual damage to an innocent viewer, there are potential crippling legal consequences for the (ir)responsible artist, as well as the inevitable loss of credibility for the field as a whole. (Remember concerns about lead in pottery glazes?)

Even though it may be easier or more accessible or cheaper to use a glass eye piece or no eye piece at all, it's wrong. In some cases, the artist simply didn't understand the dual purpose. It is inexcusable for an artist to endanger someone's vision for higher profits, or because they aren't well-informed in their chosen profession, or because it was too much trouble to add the proper safeguard. I believe that we owe the public better than this and hope that high safety standards will become common practice in kaleidoscopy.

In a similar vein, I recall an individual who taped three raw-edged mirrors together, covered the triangles with materials like foil and sold these items as kaleidoscopes. Not only does this case highlight safety concerns, but it raises other ethical issues also. Even though this individual now has upgraded scopes, that early irresponsible work eased the way to success, while other artists struggled on a less profitable path which didn't put their customers at risk.

Personal safety is an issue as well. Judy Karelitz, creator of the Karascope, believed that her fatal illness was the direct result of exposure to the plastics' solvents and related chemicals with which she worked. Judy's creative leadership is sorely missed and I hope that similar tragedies can be avoided. Do you provide safe working conditions for employees as well as yourself?

The issue of consumer safety is so clear-cut that it should be a basic industry standard. I also encourage the kaleidoscope community to more fully examine other concerns such as design and material criteria, precision and accuracy, pirating, environmental concerns, etc.

For example, if you theoretically create heirloom-quality pieces and charge heirloom-quality prices, do you fasten them mechanically rather than chemically and do you use materials and designs that will stand the test of time? If you do, some other artisan (perhaps in a hundred years) will be able to upgrade, repair or refurbish the piece as needed.

Another thorny ethical issue is the significant difference between a designer's signature line and an artist's signature on a piece of their work. That difference is blurred in this kaleidoscope renaissance, to the detriment of the public, fair directors, collectors, gallery owners and even the kaleidoscopists themselves. Although no one thinks that Liz Claibourne actually sews jeans, it *is* generally assumed that a signator artist personally created the specific piece. There are kaleidoscope lines today that are basically pre-manufactured parts, often assembled by an employee, but then represented as "created and signed by the artist." Shouldn't we distinguish between this type of item and original pieces created by the signator artist?

Precision and accuracy are of critical concern (please refer to Dr. Allen's section for a more in-depth discussion of this important issue).

Artists live or starve by their reputations, and therefore pirating of ideas, designs, marketing techniques, etc. is a very real concern. Artists need both recognition for their accomplishments and the accompanying financial benefits. Judy Karelitz, at the forefront of the new-age explosion, fought (generally unsuccessfully) to protect her ideas and creations. It's been suggested that it is unnecessary for artists to be proprietary about their work/ideas; in fact, inventors patent, authors copyright, scientists publish, etc. as a matter of course. To suggest that artists, who live by their creativity and originality, should rise above proprietary concerns is ludicrous.

The public is increasingly concerned about environmental matters. Perhaps the use of rare or non-renewable materials (e.g. some tropical hardwoods, plastics, etc.) in kaleidoscopic art could be restricted to safety features or to one-of-a-kind pieces and limited editions? For safety, there is most definitely a need to use some acrylics in scopes, but is plastic the best choice for a tube, particularly if you're covering it with other materials?

I believe that the kaleidoscope renaissance will flourish if we maintain high standards and treat our customers and colleagues as we wish to be treated.

Photographing Kaleidoscope Interiors

As you become a kaleidoscope enthusiast, you may want to be able to capture some of the exquisite images you see on film. A few pointers are in order.

The first challenge is that the eye hole of most scopes is much smaller than the lens of a camera. Only expensive micro lenses found in hospitals are capable of overcoming this barrier. The most common solution to this dilemma is to build a larger, proportional model of your mirror system to accommodate the standard camera limitations. Multiplying your mirror dimensions by about three will usually put you in range.

We suggest the following makeshift apparatus: 1) Place a large sheet of white paper on the floor; 2) place an 18" square pane of glass over the paper, supported on padded blocks or bricks; 3) place an equal square of glass over this, similarly supported; 4) stand your mirror system upright on top of this structure; 5) mount your camera on a tripod over the top of the mirrors; 6) then shine two floodlights with 75-watt bulbs on the white paper from opposite angles.

You will probably want to use a close-up lens, unless your mirrors are longer than 4 feet. 200 or 400 ASA film is advisable. Also, you should use an 80 A color balance filter to compensate for the floodlights. Set the aperture toward the small range, about f 16. This will allow for a greater depth of field. The area between the camera and the top of the mirrors must be closed to light. You can use heavy black cloth and clothespins.

The objects you choose to view ought to be proportional to the mirrors—slightly larger versions of what would normally be in the object chamber. They should be arranged on the lower pane of glass.

As you shoot, make notes of all your settings and variables. With patience and experimentation, your results will be worthwhile.

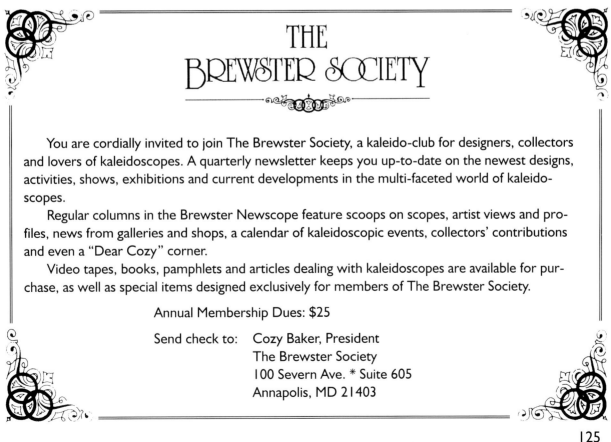

THE BREWSTER SOCIETY

You are cordially invited to join The Brewster Society, a kaleido-club for designers, collectors and lovers of kaleidoscopes. A quarterly newsletter keeps you up-to-date on the newest designs, activities, shows, exhibitions and current developments in the multi-faceted world of kaleidoscopes.

Regular columns in the Brewster Newscope feature scoops on scopes, artist views and profiles, news from galleries and shops, a calendar of kaleidoscopic events, collectors' contributions and even a "Dear Cozy" corner.

Video tapes, books, pamphlets and articles dealing with kaleidoscopes are available for purchase, as well as special items designed exclusively for members of The Brewster Society.

Annual Membership Dues: $25

Send check to: Cozy Baker, President
                  The Brewster Society
                  100 Severn Ave. * Suite 605
                  Annapolis, MD 21403

Suggested Reading

Baker, Cozy *Through the Kaleidoscope…And Beyond.* Annapolis, Maryland: Beechcliff Books, 1987.

Baker, Cozy *Kaleidorama.* Annapolis, Maryland: Beechcliff Books, 1990.

Yoder, Walter D. *Kaleidoscopes: The Art of Mirrored Magic.* Albuquerque, New Mexico: Walter D. Yoder, 1988.

Brewster, Sir David *A Treatise on the Kaleidoscope.* Edinburgh, Scotland: Archibald Constable & Co., 1819.

McClure, Don *Kaleidoscope Magic.* San Bernardino, California: Franklin Press, 1986.

Source Guide

For most materials, check with your local suppliers, such as:

Plumbing distributor
(PVC and ABS materials, copper and brass materials)

Plastics distributor
(tubing, rods, sheets)

Glass and mirror distributor
(glass discs and second surface mirrors)

Stained glass specialty shop
(materials, tools and supplies)

Paper carton and tube distributor
(packaging and tubes)

Art supply house
(mat board, papers, paints)

Craft and hobby store
(butyrate and acetate plastics, casting resin)

A current listing of sources for first surface mirrors, optical lenses and filters, brass tubes and fittings, etc. may be obtained on request. Please send a stamped, self-addressed envelope to:

Sterling Publishing Co., Inc.
387 Park Ave. South
New York, NY 10016

Cassell PLC
Villiers House
41/47 Strand
London WC2N 5JE
England

Capricorn Link Ltd.
P. O. Box 665
Lane Cove
New South Wales 2066

Kaleidoscope Artists

Audrey Barna
c/o Scherer Gallery
93 School Road West
Marlboro, NJ 07746

Alfred Brickel
Newe Daisterre Glas
13431 Cedar Road
Cleveland Heights, OH 44118

Scott Cole
7739 Michael Drive
Charlotte, NC 28215

Skeeter & Pete De Mattia
c/o Scherer Gallery
93 School Road West
Marlboro, NJ 07746

Don Doak
212 Townline Road
Harbor Springs, MI 49740

Dennis & Diane Falconer
Concept Center
RD 7, Box 71
Gibsonia, PA 15044

Amy Hnatko
4325 Locust Ave.
Cortland, NY 13045

Douglas Johnson
Windseye
10321 Indian Mound Dr.
New Port Richey, FL 34654

David Kalish
Chromascope
1933 Davis St., Suite 216
San Leandra, CA 94577

Charles Karadimos
27325 Ridge Road
Damascus, MD 20872

Dean Krause
3824 Parkhill
Ft. Wayne, IN 46805

Dorothy Marshall
P.O. Box 10855
Eugene, OR 97440

Karl Schilling
The Glass Scope
308-A Riverfront Centre
Red Wing, MN 55066

Willie Stevenson
Spirit Scopes
P.O. Box 217
Saluda, NC 28773

Credits

Project Designers:

Scott Cole - pages 68, 76, 82, 100, 108, 114

Gary Newlin - pages 64, 70

Charles Karadimos - page 94

Randy Knapp - page 86

Alfred Brickel - page 120

Network Consultants:

Ledell Murphy, Cozy Baker, Gary Newlin,
Stephen & Carmen Gallo Colley, John Cram

Technical Advisors:

Gary Newlin, Dorothy Marshall, Ethan Allen, PhD.

Index